Walaahi

A firsthand account of living through the Egyptian
Uprising and why I walked away from Islaam

Dawn Bates

© 2017 Dawn Bates

Published by Dawn Bates
www.dawnbates.com

Cataloguing-in-Publication entry is available from the British Library.

ISBN: 978-0-9957322-0-9 (paperback)
        978-0-9957322-1-6 (ebook)

Other titles by Dawn Bates:
Friday Bridge (2013)

Book cover design – Jerry Lampson
Publishing Consultant – Linda Diggle
Typeset in Baskerville 11/15pt by Author Secret

Walaahi = seriously
Pronounced: wa-lar-he

Things to note about this word:

When used at the beginning of a piece of dialogue, it has come to be known as a precursor to a lie. For example, Mubarak started his last infamous speech before his resignation with "Walaahi, Walaahi, Walaahi". Everyone who knew the subtleties of Egyptian culture knew that whatever came next, would be lies. (That doesn't mean that what you are about to read is all lies either! Kinda shot myself in the foot there, didn't I.)

Walaahi is to be an exclamation of shock or surprise both in a good way and a bad way.

Walaahi, when used amongst friends, can be used as a piece of sarcasm.

Walaahi can also be used to confirm something someone has said or done.

In a religious context, and literally, it means 'Swear to God' but for the sake of this book, I'm using the more colloquial expression of 'seriously!' Why did I use an Arabic name for my book, one that the English-speaking world wouldn't know or connect with? Well, because it just felt right. It felt right due to reasons two and three above. It felt right to use a word that Arabs across the world and those who understand languages such as Arabic and Urdu would connect with.

I also wanted to introduce the non-Arab speaking world to a word that is used so much and can bring so much joy within a conversation.

My life in Egypt was one of shock, disbelief and joy in equal measures, and I found myself using this word so much in so many different conversations, even now, after being back in the UK, it is still a word I use to this day regularly, along with many others. I flip between English and Arabic all the time and it can be something as simple as smelling cumin that makes my brain flip. It confuses a lot of people, especially when I speak with my dog Kelt in Arabic... and he understands what I'm saying. It's great having a bi-lingual dog!

Dedicated to all those who lost their lives fighting for a more humane and just Egypt, built upon equality and democracy.

Dedicated also to my two wonderful young men, Khaalid and Naasir Aysha, and Baaba, may you rest in peace always. xx

Contents

Acknowledgements

Writing this book has been an incredible journey. One of deep emotional battles, fear and a drive to make sure the truth, as I see it, is heard. A roller coaster journey for many reasons, one of self-discovery and self-belief, and incredible strength.

Living in Egypt is, at the best of times, difficult, given that martial law has been in operation since 1967. So to live there and succeed in the ways I did could only have happened with the support of Omar Aysha, Mahmoud Moussa El Tanbouly, Amira Morad, Sarah Thabit, Yasmine El Abd, Rowaida Shahwan, Sigrun Valsdottir, Gitajeli Rizk and Noha Hatem.

A special thank you goes to Dr Ramy Eissa for his amazing help and support during a very difficult and scary time in Egypt; the phone calls home to my three dear friends: Amira Adam, who sadly passed away before I returned home, may you RIP my beautiful friend, and of course the wonderful Debbie Miller and Alison Buxton. All of these wonderful people made me stronger throughout my time in Egypt.

Not forgetting my fellow author and soul sister Suzanna Egan-Mitchell, author of The Line... and owner of a fabulous scarf and red heels!

My days were given purpose and meaning, and my fight for justice and making a positive impact whilst in Egypt was driven by my love for my two sons, Khaalid and Naasir. Without you two my soul would be empty. Remember, what you think and feel is important. Use your voice. Make it heard. Use your mind, act with integrity, kindness and honour in all your daily actions.

The support I have had whilst writing this has been immense. Mahmoud, ever my biggest cheerleader. John Dunn for making me take breaks and then encouraging me to 'get on with it' when I got confronted and distracted myself with other things, cooking for me, making me endless cups of tea and taking care of my boys. Robert Kesten for honouring this book with his contribution in the Foreword. My boys for stepping up to the chores, also making me cups of tea and dinner (they are going to make such great husbands!). And, of course, Linda Diggle for encouraging me to set the deadline in place, your belief in me, and for helping me pull together the physical end product, liaising with the incredibly talented Jerry Lampson who designed the cover and who has always been a terrific support to me.

Thanks also goes to my friend and arse kicker Mr Richard Clark... he knows why ;)

I would also like to thank Julie Wells, Tina Rodgers, Rachel Walker-Morecroft, Leanne Ashworth; Rob Staff and Alan Ricahrdson (my chosen brothers); Alicia Alberley, Tonje Elisabeth Aaroe, Celeste Rains-Turk, Amith Clemence, Toni Bird and Regan Hillyer for their words of encouragement and support in the final days of this book coming together, and for cheering me on in other areas of my life.

Final thanks go to my mum, for always believing in my crazy missions and for raising me to always do my best, and not forgetting that she believes that regardless of how far I fall, or how crazy my ideas are, I will always come up smelling of roses!

I'm incredibly grateful to have you all in my life, and wish you all the very best of health, happiness and success. Lots of love to all of you.

Dawn xx

Foreword

In the summer of the Arab Spring, with tens of thousands still crowding squares in Egypt's major cities, a few of us were trying to make Alexandria a Human Rights City. There were dozens of non-profit organisations energised to move forward, many run by the extraordinary youth who saw in their actions, the possibility of a brighter future without resorting to extremism, but through increased democracy based on a human rights foundation.

At the time we asked a major internationally recognised institution to consider serving as the secretariat for the Human Rights City, they agreed to do so and we were so very close to the first city of its kind in the MENA region. Then, at the last moment, the institutional representatives said they could only do so if they had the power to determine the body of the organisation. They were informed, that to allow for that was not a democratic process and abrogated the human rights of those who did not agree with them... their response, "Don't talk to us about human rights and democracy, we've been teaching them for years."

It was then clear that a human rights city was not going to happen in Egypt, it was clear that the status quo still held the nation in its firm grip and that the "show" of the "revolution", the hope it had inspired, was a way of letting the people release decades or more of tensions and that once released, they would be easier to put back in their boxes.

The Egyptian Arab Spring **was not** a revolution; it was a management decision by the military. Since the overthrow of the king, the military has had total control of the nation. It has continued to expand its holdings and wealth and more resembles a dynasty than a force expected to protect the country from outside forces. The military owns and operates businesses and operations in ways that make it Egypt's single largest economic force.

When the protests started, as young people with no prospects and fewer possibilities arrived in Tahrir Square and other squares across the nation, they were unsure of what to demand or what was possible. Over days and weeks they were joined by Islaamists of all stripes and older people and eventually by the unions. The military was not interested in an economic shutdown and seeing that the current president had reached a level of unpopularity, it cost them nothing to end his term in office. As he was a good soldier, he turned the government over to the military... not a constitutional move, but a rational one for a man who was, in effect, a military officer.

As the protests continued and the ways and means of arriving at a "new" system with a new constitution began to play out, the army slowly became a focus of the people's anger. That was something the military didn't want, their brand was to be the protector of the people; that was how they were able to amass their fortune and maintain it without protest. So, knowing they were not prepared with a candidate, knowing no other groups, but the Brotherhood was prepared and organised for an election, they allowed the elections to go forward. They had dictated the terms and made clear that after the results, the new government would have no control over the military or the police.

For the newly elected president, he had so much to contend with he was content, at the start, to leave the military alone. On the other hand, the military regularly demonstrated their power, raising the price of fuel and other tools to remind the new government of its place in the arrangement. Now, the military was once again behind the scenes and able to control events without the wrath of the public focused on them.

As the new constitution was drafted, as the new government began to believe they were elected by the people to serve, with a mandate for their message, when they suggested a change in the military leadership, it became a threat to the nation's true rulers and they encouraged a revival of the revolution and hundreds of thousands marched on the squares again to protest the Islaamic government.

The eventual takeover by the Sisi regime was a foregone conclusion. The shutting down of organisations and institutions meant to better the lives of the people, cutting off relationships with the outside NGO world could have easily been predicted, the possibility of a Human Rights City was dashed as were human rights. Those hundreds of thousands, millions of hopeful youth saw their life blood sucked out and their futures dimmed. Numbers of these fine, bright, energised young people were silenced. Many left Egypt to work on the causes and issues they came to love during this period. Women who covered their heads and bodies uncovered and re-evaluated their relationships with family, religion and hope, and once again, went undercover as repression returned with a vengeance.

The Arab Spring should be a lesson to all of us. On one side we have the marginally successful struggle that continues in Tunisia, with almost no outside support for their experiment in democracy and citizen run government. In Egypt the tyranny continues under military dictatorship. In Syria and Libya the nations are no longer functioning as states at all; and in Jordan they remain on the edge as their larger neighbours put ever greater pressure on them, threatening their survival.

The fight to make sure every human being knows, owns and integrates human rights into their lives, taking responsibility and holding others accountable goes on... in the MENA region and around the world. The 30 articles found in the Universal Declaration of Human Rights, which will celebrate its 70th anniversary on 10 December 2018, are still the best international language and framework we have to build a sustainable world, where all people are known as equals under the law and in society. It is a cornerstone document formed by centuries of human experience and an understanding of what it is to be human in a world that always seeks to dehumanise us.

As the Arab Spring has morphed into a global battleground of growing extremism and fear, the crackdown on liberty, equality and justice mount. Governments are inclined to take the easy way out, convincing a frightened public that oppression is the only way they can be protected. Government forgets its primary role of protector and defender of their citizen's human rights, because that is harder; but harder now leads to greater success later. Nothing great in human existence has ever been easy, great art, great government, great athletes, great relationships... all these take effort and time, learning and experience and none of it is easy, but the work invested, the knowledge gained, make it all lasting.

This is not the time to take the easy way out. It is time to invest in citizens, in people, in the future. It is a time when the learning and integration of human rights into all aspects of our lives should be encouraged and introduced into all we do. We cannot rely on strongmen run governments to give us the world we want for ourselves and our children, the responsibility rests with all of us, collectively and individually. Women, men, youth and children knowing the Universal Declaration of Human Rights, as theirs, holding themselves and others accountable, will change the world.

Robert Kesten
Executive Director
PDHRE/ www.pdhre.org

PDHRE – People's Decade for Human Rights Education. PDHRE is an independent, international, non-profit making organisation, promoting, enhancing and providing learning about human rights and operates in over 60 countries.

PDHRE is convinced that imposed ignorance is a human rights violation and the learning about human rights as a way of life is an imperative for meaningful, social and economic development.

Prologue

The choice to live in Egypt had been made before ramO and I even got engaged. I had informed him that should he wish to marry me and have children with me, then we would need to live in the Middle East. The reason? Well, he is Egyptian/Palestinian.

As we couldn't live in Palestine, the only choices were Lebanon and Egypt. We knew Egypt better, even though I had a better relationship with the Aysha family in Lebanon. Lebanon had stolen my heart upon my first visit, and to be near the sea, well that just made sense to me. But ramO was a city boy, and the infrastructure was ever so slightly better in Egypt due to the amount of attacks on Lebanon by the Israeli's. It was deemed safer to live in Egypt, and be nearer to ramO's mother. Her health wasn't as great as Baaba's (my father in law, Dr Merhi Ayche) and Oman where he was based was another one of my preferred choices, not just because we would be closer to Babaa, but again due to its proximity to the sea.

We had discussed which of the three we would live in over the 14 years that led up to our move. Although I hated cities, it was time to step out of my comfort zone and embrace the madness.

It took me almost a year to pack up our home and arrange for tenants to live there. Saying goodbye to the UK was easier than I had imagined, simply because I had gotten frustrated with the breakdown in community and the increased level of racism and ignorance towards other cultures and ethnicities.

Leaving my friends was a different story, especially as they had been my lifeline over the last five years, the last four in particular with me facing my own mortality during my second pregnancy with Naasir. Debbie saved my life. Amira Adam and Ali Buxton also saved my sanity. It really is as plain and simple as that. Leaving these three behind was the hardest part of the move. But we were excited, the boys and I. ramO was apprehensive and was away working whilst I packed up the house, closed our business and dealt with all the necessaries ready to move.

As 27th July 2010 drew closer, it was time for a few leaving parties to be had, and a table-top sale by my boys in order to raise money for charity. Their parting gift. Clothes, possessions everything was either for charity shops, the table-top sale, the suitcase or the bin. The house was cleared and organised over numerous pots of coffee, Chinese takeaways from Wild Rice and lots of laughter with Amira, without whom the process would have taken a lot longer and been a lot less fun.

ramO arrived back in the UK four days before we flew to Egypt, and got stuck into sorting out his 'pile' of items to sort out, because if there was one thing I had learnt about ramO in the 15 years we were together, it was to leave him to sort out his stuff; plus I didn't want to disturb his prized games consoles that 'one day will be a lot of money'.

So with ramO having sorted out his stuff, me wandering around the home remembering all the happy and precious memories of raising our boys, endless get-togethers, parties, dinners, and general mayhem, checking all windows and doors were locked, with keys ready to hand over to the letting agent en route to the airport and the boys running around excited, it was time to head to the airport and start our new life in Egypt.

Our Arrival.

The decision to live in Egypt had been made the moment I knew I wanted to spend the rest of my life with ramO. I had told him that if we were to marry and have children then we would need to live in Egypt, especially as Palestine was a no-go area. I would have much preferred Palestine, I'm sure, but Egypt was the only safe option. I wanted to understand my future husband more and couldn't bear the thought of having children of mixed culture and languages, and not understanding the culture or speaking the language. My thinking had always been one of lead by example, and if I wasn't prepared to learn the language how could I expect my children to learn it.

Plus, having known many mixed culture and language families, the families whereby the children spoke both languages and knew the culture, the children were more confident in whom they were. I also knew it helped them to relate and connect with family members, especially cousins their own age. I didn't want a disjointed family simply because culture and language wasn't understood properly. I also didn't want to set a bad example, or cause offence to the Arabic side of the family.

Before the boys were born, I had taken Arabic lessons and continued with them until baby brain took over and my tutor moved away from the area. Unfortunately there wasn't another tutor who came anywhere close to the standard I had previously been used to. I encouraged ramO to speak with me in Arabic around the boys and to speak with them only in Arabic. He didn't and this was a bone of contention between the two of us. His boys needed to speak Arabic, we were both agreed on this, but he never took the time or made the effort to speak with them in Arabic fully, just the odd phrases.

I bought cartoon DVDs, we invested in Arabic TV satellite stations but they were as annoying as hell. Sugar-coated sickness in a way that would have even made Disney look sour. And the voices! How I wanted to throw something at the TV every time those channels were on. The programmes were of such a stark contrast from the world in which they would live in. And considering the Al Jezeera channels, children's TV, even the teenager channels were worlds apart, it was almost as if, overnight, the children would have to be ripped out of the sugar-coated lifestyle and thrown in the war-torn lifestyle. Not a healthy or wise jump for anyone! But this was the extremes of the Arab world I would get used to over the years.

After Naasir, our youngest, was born and I had recovered from his premature birth — which had seen me nearly die due to having HELLP Syndrome — I sprang into action. We had to be living in Egypt ready for Naasir to start school, and for Khaalid to absorb the language before it became more challenging than it would already be.

I gave myself 18 months to pack up the house, organise tenants whilst we were abroad, sort out all the utilities and, of course, log all my books into an excel spreadsheet. I was not going to lose any of my beloved books, or have them damaged in storage. I had spent a small fortune on investing in my knowledge from all things business, leadership and how the brain works, to religion, politics, personal development, different kinds of healing, dozens of books on health and nutrition and, of course, my classics and (auto)biographies. I logged nearly 2000 books with the help of my beloved friend Amira.

Many days and nights we would be going through every room in my home packing things into bags for charity, bags for the bin, boxes to be stored, it took us months, many pots of coffee, several Chinese meals, roast lunches, dishes of Moroccan lamb and more giggles than I had ever experienced. One of my closest friends and a true inspiration considering everything she had been through in life. Never one to play the victim card or feel sorry for herself, you could always guarantee there would be a smile on her face and a giggle session coming shortly; not to mention her fiery Scottish Yemeni temperament. When she got a bee in her bonnet, the pair of us would put the world to rights for hours, and God help anyone that crossed our paths. They would either have their ears chewed off or they'd laugh so much their sides would hurt. Either way it was pure entertainment. There was never a dull moment when Amira was around. Never.

Weeks before we were due to fly, the boys came up with an idea to sell some of the items from the house. They wanted to raise money for charity, and at the ages of three and seven, I was loving their entrepreneurial fundraising ideas. They were going to bake cakes to tempt the customers in and whilst they were also drinking tea, it gave the customers time to look at the goods and buy them. So they made signs, told everyone at nursery and school, all the neighbours and everyone in every shop we went into. They didn't hold back, and I was so incredibly proud of them. On the day of the sale, they made a princely sum of £50 and told our neighbour, Cathy, that it was for Motor Neurone Disease (MND). As someone who had MND, Cathy was very touched by this and told them to keep half the money and she would pay the other half. The boys left the money with her and were so excited. They were going to buy lots of things when they got to Egypt because £25 was 250LE – and that was a lot of money.

They were so excited about what they had done, they told An'na[1] (my mother-in-law) who always knew how to burst someone's bubble. She was horrified that I had allowed them to sell our things in the street. What would the neighbours think? That we were so poor we had to sell our things? There was simply no reasoning with her. She couldn't see the selfless, beautiful gesture the boys had come up with, nor could she see the entrepreneurial spirit they had. Khaalid wasn't perturbed and eagerly told Gidu[2] (my father-in-law) who was incredibly proud of the boys and gave them an additional £10 for their efforts. At this point both the boys started shouting, "AWESOME!!" and agreed to give Cathy next door another £10 and split the other £10 between them both.

I cried tears of pride. Here were my two little boys selflessly giving to help others. It was an emotional time anyway, moving home, leaving friends behind, everything I knew. I was excited, nervous and yet very sad to be leaving. Yet I knew this would be great for us, for all the family.

Leaving day had finally arrived. Our home had tenants arriving in a couple of weeks, everything was in storage and there were still a few bits and pieces left in the house, which the cleaning firm would be removing. We had simply run out of time. There were a few crossed words between ramO and I because he hadn't done the things he said he would do, but a few phone calls were made and these would be rectified as we landed in Cairo Airport.

---

1   An'na – the term used for Grandma. Comes from Turkish routes but is used within Egypt.

2   Gidu – the term used for Grandpa/Granddad.

The drive to the airport was loaded with emotions. I had never lived outside of the UK before, yes I'd travelled extensively, but never lived anywhere but England. I felt confident though. I had been part of the Arab and Muslim world for almost 20 years. I knew the family. I had friends there and, me being me, I knew I'd make new ones.

I was also confident in the boys enjoying their new lives. They were great boys, still are. They took everything in their stride and just got on with it. My mother-in-law had arranged for them to start at Sahara International School. We just had to sort out certain bits of paperwork in the first couple of weeks and they would start at the same time as everyone else.

Our apartment was also sorted, it was one of my mother-in-laws, and overlooked the Nile. Nothing really needed doing, all we had to do was sort out visas and begin our new life in Egypt.

The boys and I would learn more of the culture and language on a much deeper level. My months of planning had paid off. I was exhausted, but relieved to be going. I had had enough of many things in the UK and just needed a break from it all. I couldn't wait to fall into my new bed and sleep.

I read a book and slept a little on the plane whilst the boys and ramO played on the Nintendo DS's. As we landed, in true Egyptian Air style, a huge round of applause was given to the pilot for a safe landing. This had always made me chuckle and Naasir being Naasir said, "What are they clapping for mummy? Did they think it was going to crash?"

I told him to ask Baaba, he would explain, as it is the only airline I had ever travelled on whereby the passengers would always clap the pilot.

In true Egyptian style the airport was disorganised and busy. Workers were attempting to take our luggage away from us in exchange for a tip, but I had learnt early on during my travels to Egypt that you do not let them take your luggage. I said, "la3 shukrun," meaning, "No, thank you." Coming from an obviously white woman always came as a bit of a shock to them. Still, it had the desired effect, if not the first time then most certainly the second time I said it.

Leaving the airport was, again, a nightmare. People everywhere and the heat hitting me like I'd just been stuck in a pre-heated oven. I had never been able to adjust to the heat of Egypt in the middle of July. I was more of a spring and autumn girlie back home in the UK, so arriving in the middle of July had been solely on the necessity of schooling issues.

I was, however, looking forward to my first winter in Egypt. Still, I had to focus on the here and now and just get through the airport to the taxi with both boys and husband in tow, without losing any of them in the mass of people.

Once in the taxi, I started to relax. I was used to the crazy driving, the five members of a family all riding along on a motorbike, with no crash helmets and the youngest child being carried under the arm of the mother, with the middle child sat between her and the father with the eldest child sat on the handle bars at the front. This no longer phased me. Neither did the eight or nine year old driving a large trailer, led by a donkey, carrying a huge supply of vegetables through the Cairo ring roads.

All of these sights reminded me I was home. My second home. My chosen home. Cairo, Egypt was the place I had chosen to live. No one made me live there. It was completely my choice, and I was going to give it my best shot. Being a country girl from a small village called Friday Bridge on the Norfolk/ Cambridgeshire border, living in London was a nightmare for me, and yet here I was moving to the fourth largest city in the world, with a very different climate and culture, with a population of 20 million people. It was going to be great. It was going to be the best move we'd ever made.

We pulled up in Ma'adi and drove into the carpark of the compound where there were six 25 story apartment buildings. I felt dizzy just looking up, and also very relieved that the apartment wasn't in a typical ex-pat compound. I was not up for the "us and them" mentality. I wanted to live amongst the Egyptians. I was a mother of two Egyptian Palestinians, the wife of an Egyptian Palestinian. We were not going to live in an ex-pat compound and separate ourselves from the very people we had gone to Egypt to learn from.

As we arrived at the fifth building into the compound, we were met by the ba'waab[3] of the buildings, who offered to help carry our bags. This, I allowed. I couldn't offend the ba'waab on the first meeting now, could I?

He took us up to the apartment and showed me, not ramO, just me, how to operate the gas bottle for the oven in the kitchen. This was a sign of things to come, so I called ramO in and asked him to understand what the ba'waab was saying and then explain it to me. He refused, saying I had to learn to tune into the language now we were living in Egypt.

So, I listened, and thought, *You know what, I think I get it.* Feeling slightly confident, I mean, I had been camping before and used a gas cylinder and

---

3   Ba'waab – caretaker of the building

camping stove, how different could this be? So, in desperate need of a coffee, I filled the kettle with water from the filtered tap, and turned the gas on ready to light the hob; and hey presto I did it! I was so excited I jumped up and down clapping my hands. I was so proud of myself. I had actually understood the ba'waab.

Next, it was on to dinner. I wasn't going to spend my first night cooking on the hob, so it was just going to have to be roasted veg and chicken, which ramO went out to get. He was back in less than 10 minutes, so with all the veg chopped up and chicken ready to go, I set to lighting the oven. Carefully turning the gas on, and lighting the match and KABOOM!!! A massive roll of flames came out of the oven, ramO came running into the kitchen with the boys not far behind and I'm standing there checking my eyebrows are still intact. All I could smell was burnt hair and I was not pleased. I wasn't really bothered about the kitchen, but my eyebrows... you bet I was worried about them! Call me shallow, but I like my eyebrows, I wanted to keep my eyebrows.

Thankfully, everything was okay and apparently, it is normal for the first lot of gas to come out of one of the gas bottles like. Thanks for the heads up ramO! So, coffee on the go, dinner in the oven and now I could ring my mum and let her know we were in the apartment safe and well – albeit nearly with singed eyebrows – but at least it gave her something to giggle about.

I fell asleep before dinner was ready, so as soon as we'd eaten and I'd made the bed, I climbed in and slept. I was shattered. Little did I know this was going to be an on-going state of being for a good while yet!

Our first month.

Waking up I was a bit disorientated, especially as I had been woken throughout the night by gunfire. The first time it happened I thought at first it was the bird scarer's I had grown up listening to as a child out in the fields behind my childhood home. But something inside me told me this wasn't right.

I woke ramO up and told him I heard gunfire. He told me not to worry and go back to sleep. It was just the people in the area nearby. I asked what he meant and he dismissed it, telling me to go back to sleep. I was awoken a few more times that night by the sound of guns going off, hoping it wouldn't be a regular occurrence.

When I woke up for breakfast the boys and ramO were already up and making breakfast. It was such a treat, especially as ramO had been working away in Zurich and I had been dealing with all the move, closing our businesses and dealing with the boys.

They had already been over to the local shop and purchased everything we needed. Nagwa, the mother-in-law, had stocked the cupboards with tinned and dried foods, as well as some teabags. But I needed coffee, and fresh foods; especially as sardines are not my thing and the dried foods would need soaking for at least a day before cooking.

I probed further about the gunfire in the night. ramO told me that there was a low class area next to the compound, which is very common, and sometimes the men fire guns into the air, even more so when there is a wedding going on. He said I'd know when there was a wedding going on, because the music would be loud.

That night I found out exactly what he meant; I also understand how the traditional Arabic music has developed his taste for techno. The bass lines and the pace were certainly getting me into the mood of going raving, and I even sent a friend, Mark, a message saying he should get his arse over to Cairo to join in the party!

Throughout the first day we spent the time going through how things would pan out in the first couple of weeks and what was needed for the boys schooling. There were uniforms to be purchased, residential visas to be obtained, legal documentation to sort out, so it was decided that ramO would go and sort out all the legalities and I would stay home with the boys organising the apartment, stocking up the cupboards and getting to know the local area.

ramO left shortly after breakfast and the boys and I set about sorting out the apartment. It needed a good clean as the dust had settled, so that was the first task.

The boys then took me to the local shop they had been to earlier in the morning with ramO so I could see what else was needed for the week. I bought loads of veg and some basterma[4]. Knowing that I didn't have to travel from Sheffield to London to get basterma was such a joy. Here it was right on my doorstep. My life has always been about enjoying the simple things in life, and this smoked, cured beef was one of my favourite meats. Absolutely perfect for breakfast, a light lunch or adding to roasted veg. As the Greeks say, "Bacon is not meat, it's seasoning."

I was pleased with the results the boys and I had created cleaning the apartment, getting it ready for when our things finally turned up. Beds were sorted, clothes were put away and tea had been made.

When ramO got back he was impressed, stressed, but impressed. I made him tea and asked how he'd got on. He showed me a load of paperwork and as he'd been out in the heat all day, I told him to get some rest and I would fill in the paperwork, as much as I could. He commented on how good the apartment looked and had one of those grins on his face that I knew hid something he would later explain if I hadn't already guessed it. When I asked what he was grinning about, he told me I would know by the morning, and know in the morning I did!

Having spent a good three hours cleaning the day before, waking up to see

---

4   Basterma – Egyptian cured sliced beef

the dust all over everything again, I was shocked. It was as if I hadn't done anything. I now felt disappointed in myself for being critical of the mother-in-law as I thought she had not bothered to clean the apartment before we'd arrived. I quickly realised this is why so many of our friends had maids, constantly had the air conditioning on, and never opened the windows. Keeping your home dust free and clean in Egypt was a mammoth task, so my absolute respect goes out to all those families who do not have a maid.

I spent about three hours a day cleaning the apartment and felt like I wasn't getting anywhere. I wanted to get on with other things, and had other things to be getting on with, like dealing with a problem that had arisen with one of the banks back home.

Due to a clerical error made by one of the counter staff, I was unable to access my bank account, either online or by phone, even though I passed all the security checks, could tell the people on the phone all the payments going in and out of the account, they still wouldn't allow me to do anything. It was really frustrating, and would cause me a lot of problems when I returned back to the UK. I just had to leave it and deal with it when I returned; whenever that would be.

Going to the local shops was an interesting experience. I was used to the locals staring at me in Fagala[5] and around the less touristic areas of Cairo, but this was taking things to a whole new level. It was as if the boys and I had landed from outer space with multiple heads. ramO had not prepared me for the cultural difference in this part of Ma'adi. It was very different to the rest of Cairo I had experienced before; I was told that Ma'adi had many ex-pats, still local, as neither of us wanted to live in a total ex-pat location – I mean, what is the point of living in a different country if you don't mix with the locals, learn the language, the customs, eat the food etc? For me, you might as well stay in your own country.

Integration is essential, and especially so for me and my family as we had three predominant cultures at play. This part of Ma'adi was very close to a beladi area[6] which backed onto a local place called Dar al salaam (Place of peace) and this was a slum which had grown so quickly, and trust me, a place

5   Fagala – an area within Ramsis where Nagwa, the mother-in-law lived and the boys first went to the Sahara International School

6   Beladi - local low class people, mainly non educated and living in either the countryside or if within the cities, in very poor conditions, almost like slums.

of peace it was not! I knew I didn't want to live here in this area for much longer. It wasn't somewhere that my energy suited. It was not the location I wanted to raise my children, nor was it a place I could relax into. It just wasn't me.

Don't get me wrong, after a while I got to know the local shop owner and the ba'waab of our building and the compound, but saying good morning, or rather 'saba el kheir' to those living nearby was not a good idea; for me this went against everything I knew. I am a friendly person, grew up in the countryside so saying 'good morning/afternoon/night' was part of me. It is something I have experienced a lot in my travels across Europe in the smaller towns and villages, so to not be able to say 'Good morning' to my neighbours felt wrong.

If I said 'Saba el kheir!' to even the people I saw regularly, they would look at me really offended, especially the women. The men were just *too* over friendly with it and so I just didn't bother in the end. It just wasn't worth it. The only people I said Saba el Kheir to was Abd'Dullah and Ma3'waan. They both worked in the shop and helped me improve my Arabic with new phrases that were more local, rather than using the Arabic I had learnt from text books and from other areas of the Arab world.

I was soon able to come up with my own phrase, "Ana 3a'ndik shorba 3arabi min 3arabi dunnya fi mukhti." (I have Arabic soup from around the Arab world in my brain.)

When Abd'Dullah and Ma3'waan heard me say this the first time they burst out laughing and replied, "Inti asal ya habibiti." (You are sweet, my beloved.) They were impressed with my Arabic skills and at the speed at which I was picking it up, as well as making my Arabic more Egyptian. I was beginning to understand the Arabic I had been learning in the UK and from friends, wasn't serving me well in Egypt.

It was making me stand out more than my linen trousers, chiffon tops over vest tops, Birkenstocks and Chanel shades were. I learnt to adapt my clothing, tone it down a bit. I was still wearing my own clothes but it was the way I wore them that changed. I also bought much lighter clothing, because man was it hot! I had only been there a few days when I had started looking forward to October when the temperature would start to drop! But hey, what did I expect, I had chosen to live in a desert country, a lot closer to the equator.

One of the biggest discomforts about our new life in Egypt was getting to the train station. We were about an hour's walk, which is not normally a problem for me, but we had to walk through Dar El Salaam, avoiding donkey droppings, being followed, inappropriate comments, loads of rubbish on the floor – you couldn't really call them streets because they weren't, more of a dirt track.

ramO had also told us not to speak English at all. Just the four of us walking together through the area was drawing attention because not only did none of us wear the gallebeya[7]'s but we were a mixed race family, all with different skin tones, me being the fairest, then Naasir being a little darker, then Khaalid and then ramO. We walked through this area many times and I soon had the route memorised. I just had to build up the confidence to walk through it alone. Something I was not looking forward to. If the comments, men following us and the staring were this bad with ramO and the boys, I dreaded to think what it would be like by myself.

I soon found out, and learnt a new word very quickly, "3a'iib!" Which means, "Shame on your culture!" This has probably been the most powerful word I could have learnt and shocked many into lowering their gaze and leaving me alone, along with the odd round of applause from the older generation of locals.

One time, after I had been walking through Dar El Salaam for about a month on my own, a group of young lads following me through, calling me 'abyaad', ' habibiti asal', 'ya sit'ti' and 'mu'oza'.

I turned and stood my ground and shouted, "Wallahi?? 3a'iib!! Inta owza ragul btkelim ya mama dah?" Which translates to, "Seriously!? Shame on your culture!! Do you want the men to speak with your mother like this?" At which point several ladies and much older men sitting around smiled at me and nodded their agreement with comments of "aiwa, 3a'iib!" (Yes, shame on your culture!). These lads were shocked and backed off, especially after an elderly man who could hardly walk came out with his walking stick held high in the air shaking it at them.

From that day onwards, I grew in confidence, and smiles from the women on the path through Dar El Salaam for days after this incident told me they had heard about what had happened. I started to relax and enjoy walking through. I felt accepted by them, and safer. It had only taken me a few weeks,

---

7   Gallebeya – the long dress that both men and women wear in the Arab world. The women mostly wear the black ones, with men wearing the white/cream ones

and I'd already discovered quicker, more direct routes through to the train station; and to be honest, I really do believe the experience of living so close to such a poor area taught me so much about the intense juxta-positioning of the wealthy and the incredibly poor across Egypt.

It taught me more humility than I have ever known. Taught me to be more grateful, accepting of others and less judgmental. I began to understand how the family and social status we are born into is pure chance; unless you believe that we get to choose our parents before we are born from a generational transcendence point of view.

Living next to such a poor area really got me present to how even though we had all the trappings of the upper middle class lifestyle, none of it actually mattered. The people with very little education, very few possessions were wealthier than many of us who have degrees, an abundance of possessions and homes across the globe. Living this close to poverty really brought the phrase, "Some people are so poor, all they have is money," crashing down on me.

In Egypt there isn't really the segregation of lower, middle and upper class living in different areas like we have in the UK, everyone is thrown in together in Egypt, part of which does create many of the problems, but solves probably as many as it creates. Don't get me wrong, there are the wealthy areas of Cairo, with brand new gated communities on the increase on the outskirts of Cairo, such as T'Gamma Khaimis and T'Gamma Ow'l (5th Settlement and 1st Settlement), but they all come with a very low class area very close by for all the drivers, maids and ba'waab's to live in.

I told ramO that I had no intention of living in one of these gated settlements as I had gone to Egypt to integrate, learn about the culture, the foods and the people. He assured me we wouldn't live in one of these settlements as they ranged from £2-3 million plus – way out of our price range. The more I explored the more I fell in love with Egypt. Yes, I hated the smelly streets – especially the urine stench in Ramsis Square – and the rubbish piles on the side of the streets. But there was just something about Egypt that got under my skin. I can't explain it, but as the Egyptian's say, "Once you've drank from the Nile, you're Egyptian." – not that I actually drank from the Nile itself directly, I don't think I would be here writing this book if I had, but I'm sure you get the drift.

The biggest thing for me was the heat; it was just too much for me during the day, and I found that I would want to be sleeping all the time. The heat made me so lethargic I found I always had an afternoon nap – a nanna nap as my friend, Rowaida, called them, and although I love my sleep, I love being active more. Creating stuff, producing results, exploring my surroundings, I only live once and wasting my time sat around or sleeping just doesn't work for me.

One of my favourite things to do was to watch the beladi children, whether it was working to help out their family and bring in the money, or simply playing with anything they could find. They were happy with nothing and incredibly creative with how they played and spent their time.

A far cry from the children in the UK who, if they didn't have an X-Box or TV to watch, or the latest toy, would moan they were bored or had nothing to do, even though their bedrooms were probably piled high with toys and activities.

It was also really interesting to watch how resilient these kids were and just how spoilt and pampered the kids in the UK had become. This is when I coined the phrase "bubble wrap parenting" – whether it was the middle to upper classes in Egypt or at home in the UK, so many are becoming scared of life itself and are decreasing their comfort zones based on rules and regulations dictated by the government or insurance companies, led by the Health and Safety Executive. My mind whirred at how much talent and work ethic we had already lost in the UK due to the insurance companies dictating when kids are allowed to get a Saturday job, and how we should all live our lives, just because of some risk assessment a group of people had completed from their own very small comfort zone. The insaneness of the Health and Safety Executive has made pretty much anything normal into a high risk.

Take climbing trees, for example. Kids are not allowed to climb trees in school grounds, parks or other public places, just in case they fall. Yet they are allowed to climb a metal or concrete structure that has been made to a specific height, weight and a whole host of other parameters. What these all-knowing executives have failed to realise, though, is that when a child climbs a tree, not only are they connected to the energy of that tree and nature itself, feeling the natural texture, but the child is learning to balance on a much deeper level, using their core muscles in a way that a sturdy structure cannot give them. When a child climbs a tree, the child is doing more risk assessments, using their skill and wit a lot more than with a solid concrete or metal structure, simply because the tree is fluid, either with the flexible branch, or the wind. They also forget that trees are super cool and a great hiding place for games of hide-and-seek. Sometimes I wonder how on earth we all managed to survive the millennia that we have been in existence. But I digress; expect it to happen throughout this book.

In between sleeping and watching how people went about life from a new perspective, there were still the issues of sorting out school uniforms, visas and a whole host of other insane paperwork. ramO had the task of going to the various government buildings to deal with the blinkered officials and mountains of red tape, whilst I went to the school shop to deal with the school uniforms. An easy task, or so I thought. Not only were all the uniform sizes ridiculously tiny waisted and long-legged, the quality of the material wasn't what I was expecting. Another reminder of the quality of life we have in the UK.

The ladies in the school shop were very helpful and we did manage to sort out the uniforms, but not without having to take the clothes to a tailor to amend the trousers. ramO was able to join me and the boys in the shop towards the end as many of the offices he had been told to visit, had managed to avoid taking responsibility and told him to go to another office, which was closed; he had to go back another day when someone else would be able to deal with the issues at hand.

My admiration for him was growing. There was no way I would have been able to deal with the heat, the amount of unhelpful mewazaafeen[8] and the number of restrictions that had been implemented due to the dictatorial control from above, one that I would learn very quickly is deeply ingrained into the mindset of the people in all areas of life.

The time came, though, when I did have to deal with the stupidity of 'the system' when Khaalid was placed in Year One, when he should have been placed in Year Three. There had been a misunderstanding with regards to his year group as he had attended a private school in the UK, which uses a different system to state schools, which is different again to the American system of grading year groups. What was more surprising for me was the fact that even though the head teacher knew how old Khaalid was, had the comparison grid of international schooling year groups right in front of her, and knew her own school administration had make a mistake when processing the paperwork, she still couldn't grasp the full extent of the situation and refused to put Khaalid

---

8   Mewazaaf – literally means employee but is known throughout Egypt to mean a government employee. The plural of this is mewazaafeen. If we wanted to be exact about the official name, we would use mewazaaf 7akooma meaning government employee. (7 = h in franco Arabic)

in the correct year group. When I flipped the age groups to Khaalid being placed into a year group two years above, knowing it was equally unsuitable, I received a death stare from the head teacher because she finally realised the absurdity of the situation (even though, looking back with hindsight, Khaalid being in a year group two years older than him in that school would have probably turned out better for him).

We left the meeting with the head teacher having got nowhere. This meant more visits to mogamma3[9] for ramO. I couldn't believe the hassle this was causing and even though ramO was explaining what was going on when he came back to our apartment, it was still a square peg in a round hole in my brain. Nothing had any logic to it and was wasting so much time. Add to this the heat of July and this made for a quite irritable ramO... and who could blame him. Here we were starting life as a family in a country he had left nearly 20 years earlier due to the ridiculousness of the government and the people, and nothing had changed, if anything, it had gotten worse.

He came back one day and we discussed what the next step would be. We agreed I'd go along with him to the mogamma3 building – add a bit of pressure as a British mother, a Muslim revert, an author – the prestige element, because if there is one thing the Egyptians love its prestige, especially when there is the khawaaga[10] element to it.

So the next day we set off to the mother-in-law's to drop the boys off with her and headed to the mogamma3 building. We walked up nine flights of stairs to sit in an office with more desks and filing cabinets than I had ever seen in one room in my life. People smoking and no air conditioning, at least eight high piles of paperwork on each desk – the complete opposite of my 'clear desk, clear mind' policy in my businesses. No confidentiality, no organisation, nothing to stop paperwork going missing and getting lost.

After sitting in this office for what was close to an hour, we were then told we needed to go to another building about 15 minutes walk away. Once there, we had to wait another 30 minutes for the person to return to their office, to be told we needed to go back to where we had just come from.

When we arrived back at mogamma3 we had to sit outside an office waiting for the woman that was in charge of school placements in Egypt.

---

9   Mogama3 - the national government offices surrounding Tahrir Sqaure

10   Khawaaga – foreigner – as used in khawaaga syndrome – being friends with a foreigner just to enjoy reflective glory. Akin to the hangers on in 'society' circles.

Upon walking into her office the first thing we saw was a really large portrait of Hosni Mubarak up on the wall… just a 'subtle' way of reminding all mewazaaf who's in charge, and not to step out of line, or use initiative, which of course no one did. Egypt is a dictator-led country, after all.

Sitting there listening to the Arabic being spoken, I could pick only bits out of it due to the speed at which the talking was happening. I could see ramO getting more and more frustrated so I stepped in and asked what was going on. He explained to me that this woman in charge was refusing to move Khaalid into the correct year group until the end of the year. Well, at this point, I kinda flipped. I was hot, thirsty, tired and completely pissed off at the level of stupidity I was seeing around this whole situation. So I let rip and basically told her that the reason why Egypt was suffering from a brain drain of its best minds was because of this level of stupidity from people that were in charge; not to mention how the second most used word in Qur'raan was ilm[11] and she was showing none of it. I then asked her how she expected her country to flourish if here she was with all the evidence she needed that a simple mistake had happened, and all she was required to do was sign a piece of paper for it to be corrected. How did that fit into the teachings of the Qur'raan? When I then said, "Ya haram," her eyes finally tipped into aggression towards me as I ended with, "Yes, I know you understand English, and have understood every word I have said. Now please sign the paperwork and give it to us so we can take it back to the school, and enable our child to learn and prosper. And if you are a mother, you will understand my desire to educate my child. We came to live here so our children could connect with Egypt and Egyptians, connect with his Arab identity and this is how you treat us? 3'iib!".

During this time ramO was saying, "Babe, shhh!" but I didn't care. I wanted my child in school to learn and make friends here in Egypt, and if that meant fighting with this woman in true Egyptian-mother style then I would. I'd seen and heard enough from my mother-in-law's discussion to know how things got done in this country. If you wanted anything done, you either had to kiss people's backsides, or fight… and there was no way I was going to kiss this woman's backside, especially when she sat there with her arrogance overflowing in abundance simply because of the position she held in the government. No one messes with my boys. No one.

---

11   Ilm – wisdom

At this point she said something to ramO that I didn't understand, to which he chuckled at and smiled, and then nodded at me before signing the piece of paper and then handing it to us. We then left with a response of, "Shukrun.[12]" and headed home.

Whilst walking home I asked ramO what she had said to him at the end. He told me that she had said I had made my points very clearly, and had fought my case like a true Egyptian woman, but I wouldn't get very far if I kept reminding people of their Islaamic duties; I had to learn to hold my tongue. ramO's chuckle was confirmation that he knew me holding my tongue would never happen. It had rarely happened before, so why would I change something that had served me pretty well up until now? I wouldn't.

Now for all you office workers in the western world, to really understand what it is like working in one of these government offices, just try this little exercise. I want you to imagine your day. You wake up, get dressed and all that jazz, head off to work on the tube/metro/underground where you have to push your way on, and once you are on, you have no space to move. You push your way off the tube/metro/underground and head to your office through the crowded streets, filled with rubbish, and arrive at your office hot and sweaty.

There are no water coolers or coffee machines. If you are lucky your office may have a chap that fetches and carries for everyone, so he may be able to go and get you something. Now imagine the phones and PCs have been taken away from you, your desk is stacked with four to five piles of paper, about the size of seven to eight reams of copier paper.

Now picture another five to ten desks, with the above amount of paper on them, in your office, with a filing cabinet for each desk... feeling a little cramped? Well now add three to four wall fans, increase the heating to about 30 degrees celsius, and work. Remember though, you are in a high rise building and the lifts are not working so you have to walk up four flights of stairs. Due to no phones, colleagues are shouting information around the offices. You are working on a case and you need one of the papers you are working on approved by your colleague in the next building.

So, you now have to walk all the way down the stairs, into the crowded streets (imagine London rush hour, all day, times six) to the building next door to see your colleague on the sixth floor. Again, the lift is not working so

---

12   Shukrun – thank you

you will have to walk up the stairs. You get there and your colleague has had to go to another building to get something else sorted out, and will be back in 30 minutes, which turns into an hour (if you are lucky).

You have to wait because you cannot complete your work until it is done.

Your colleague turns up, approves the document (again if you are lucky and there are no missing stamps/translations etc), and you have to make your way back to your office, all the way up the stairs again to your desk whereby you can finish the task in hand. Just to get an approval signature on a document you have just lost two to three hours. Imagine this scenario with everything you do, all day, every day. This is an average working day for the Egyptians in the government, and many other Egyptian companies.

Now, I want you to imagine how you would feel knowing that although you have been employed to do a job, you know you have the skills and the knowledge to do it well, but you are not free to develop new ideas, improve your working environment and think freely. You just have to do what the Big Boss wants, who by-the-way, has no idea about the issues you, and your hundreds of colleagues face daily. If you even so much thought about challenging a process or suggested a new way of doing something, you could lose your job.

People are in abundance in Egypt and there is always someone to replace you. You work in very poor conditions for very little money, and you are surviving the system each day. You know that the Dictator is spending millions on shopping malls for the foreigners. You know he has spent millions on the Tourist Police stations. And yet, here you are in a run-down, broken building, with no systems to improve simple communication between departments, to streamline efficiency, to share best practice and to record all the information to make searching for your case loads easier and quicker, not to mention improve your working life, and the lives of your fellow countrymen. No way of making a difference. You are just a cog in a very big broken wheel.

If you do what is right, take initiative and sort the paperwork out later, not only could you be sacked, but you would never get a job again. What do you do? You give in and comply. You become scared of doing what you know is right, you become frustrated and then you just comply. A nasty and corrupt way of breaking people; a mind-controlling and soul-destroying system; a system I cannot, and will not, respect.

The people of Egypt, I have to respect. They have lived under occupation and dictatorships for a few hundred years now; I know that the people of England would not be able to deal with even a quarter of what the Egyptians have to deal with, especially the people of my generation and younger. I know I could not deal with the struggle and frustrations on a daily basis. I also knew there was no way I would want a job working for someone else in Egypt, but then why would I work? I had come to Egypt to take some time off, to spend with the family. My mind was whirring, all of these ideas on how to improve this system were flying around in my head. My business brain was not switching off.

I needed to chill out and relax, so we collected the boys from the mother-in-law's and went back to our apartment. I was shattered but sleeping wasn't an option. I needed to cook dinner, and there was still a load of stuff to get sorted, like chasing up the shipping company to find out where out things were. Already a month late and I was getting frustrated. I wanted to settle, I wanted to make my mother-in-laws Louis XVI style, gold everything, apartment into something I could call our home; a challenge in itself as she had placed so many restrictions on us as to what was allowed and not allowed to be moved or packed away, it was more than suffocating. But hey, beggars can't be choosers as they say.

Whilst chopping the veg for dinner, I started to really get present to what it was we had done. The enormity of ramO moving back to Egypt, my dream of living in Egypt, one of the holy lands of the Prophets, the 'Mother of the World' or 'Um Dunnya' as the Egyptians like to call it. The heat, the politics, the lack of systems, broken streets, rubbish everywhere you turned, harassment at every turn, the schooling and living in one of the mother-in-law's apartments.

I needed a game plan. I needed to figure out a way of being able to live in this chaos and remaining sane. My head started spinning, I needed air. The kitchen didn't have a window so I went into the bathroom and stood with my head out of the window in there. Then I looked down. We were 16 floors up. Then my mind went somewhere it really shouldn't have. I added the average number of people per apartment per floor, then multiplied that by the number of floors in the building. My knees buckled. My head spun. There were more people in this building alone than in Friday Bridge, the village I had grown up in. I sat down. Then another calculation happened, I multiplied that number to the number of buildings in our compound, and realised there were more people within this small compound that there was in the small town and three surrounding villages nearest Friday Bridge. My head spun again, so I called ramO, made sure he had the boys settled, locked the bathroom door and we had a spliff. I needed to relax. Needed to clear my head.

Whilst having the spliff we both explored ways of us being able to relax, the first thing that came to my mind was the feluccas[13]. I needed to get on the water. I needed to hear the water. So after dinner we headed down the corniche to the Ma'adi felucca station and spent the next hour on the felucca. It was bliss. For the first time since being in Egypt, I was relaxing. There was just me and my boys, on a sailing boat, enjoying the peace and quiet of the Nile, with just the water lapping up against the side. The boys were playing with ramO and I was staring out into the distance; my mind just releasing the negativity of the day, watching the sky as it turned dark, then closing my eyes and just feeling the night air on my face, smiling to myself because it was still really hot and here we were on a felucca, on the Nile, at night.

As I opened my eyes, I looked over at the boys and ramO and knew in that moment I had to go on a felucca at least once a week. It was going to be my go-to place. A space where I could journal, plan, write and just be. Being on the water, on the beach, in the sea or the swimming pool has always served my mind, body and soul well.

I thought back to being on the beach in the UK, especially the times of being on the beach at night with my mum and dad fishing. Hearing the crash of the waves on the beach, looking out seeing all the boats way off into the distance, wanting to be out there; surrounded by the ocean, on the way to somewhere with no rush, no traffic, just the ocean all around and the sky above.

I felt something in that moment. I felt something shift. A longing to be at sea. Like I had experienced when I was growing up, but this time it was more powerful. It was a deep hunger, like the Viking in me waking up after centuries of sleeping. A shiver ran through my body, goosebumps rose across my skin and excitement ran through me with a little giggle escaping. I knew I had to feed this hunger. I knew I had to make this long lost dream come true. Then I closed my eyes, dropped my head back over the side of the felucca and smiled to myself. Tears escaped my eyes and I knew that this would have to be something I did by myself because ramO wouldn't want that life. He

---

13   Felucca – small sailing boat on the Nile which seats up to 10-14 people

was a city boy, very much feet firmly on the ground. But we'd make it work. We always made everything work. It's what we did.

I started running, albeit around the carpark surrounding the seven buildings in the compound. There was nowhere else for me to run at night, and there was no way I was running during the day! In that heat! You must be joking! I could only just function in the heat! I started to gain an audience which I found more amusing than daunting, well, in the beginning. After a few weeks, my running sessions got easier as the temperature at 10pm at night dropped from 35 degrees!! My goal was to be running 15 miles a week before the year is out (that's not the calendar year, that's summer to summer!) In the UK, a three mile run was not an issue for me, but here, even after a 15 minute run, the dust and sand attacked my nose and throat, which in turn makes it hard to breathe. Learning a safe route, or settling for a treadmill, was the initial hurdle, and once I was over that, the running would become enjoyable again.

Over the next few weeks we ploughed through all the bureaucratic red tape, and dealt with the long list of school supplies for each of the boys. I had never seen, or heard of anything like it. We had to provide them with all their copy books, the stationary, tissues, wet wipes, anti-bacterial gel along with a whole host of other items. Having sent the boys to a private school in the UK where everything was provided, I wondered why these weren't provided for.

I did the maths of how much roughly the school was making just with entrance fees, then calculated the overheads for a school, and there was absolutely no reason why the monies paid in fees shouldn't have covered the cost of all these materials; especially when the school would be able to bulk buy, bringing down the price. My business brain kicked in. I started to do the maths and projections of the income. It was sound. I didn't understand why such a simple solution of calculating all costs wasn't completed and fees set accordingly.

When I spoke with friends who had children in both state and private school systems around the world, we shared a few moments of amused disbelief, and not just about that, about many aspects of Cairo life. I was beginning to realise how sheltered ramO and his mum had kept me from the reality of Egyptian life on the many visits over the previous 15 years. I was getting a reality check, on many things.

There were many items on the list that I didn't send the boys with, such as the anti-bacterial wipes AND gel, the tissues, the endless amounts of stationary, when half of it would do. I've never been one for bubble wrap parenting and often make the observation that it's amazing how long humans managed to survive climbing trees, camping wild, exploring and riding horses, basically being outdoors, having fun and getting down and dirty with nature.

Don't get me wrong I'm saying there isn't a risk of getting sick when outdoors in a city such as Cairo, the third most populated city in the world, next to New York and Mexico City, home to over 7.7 million residents, and they are the people the government have registered, but over-sanitising is not something I subscribe to. It destroys our immune system and prevents us from overcoming illnesses that our bodies have fought off since we lived in caves.

Shortly after the boys had started school in the September, ramO and I started figuring out what we were going to do. We'd spoken about it before we had left the UK. It would be easier for him to get work due to him speaking both Arabic and English. Plus, he knew his way around more.

I wanted to write my first book and take time out with the boys. The last year had been an incredibly hectic time with the boys whilst ramO had been working away in Luxembourg, Switzerland and London.

We hadn't sat down together and thrashed it all out, which, as it happens, worked out better as I'd had an awakening. I wasn't the same woman I had been stepping onto that plane. What I had seen and experienced already in the first three months was like a right hook to the cheekbone and almost a total knockout. I remember lying on the bed with my left hand on my forehead and my right hand on my abdomen and tears rolling down my face. In part relief that we had done it. We'd spoken about it ever since we got together. It was actually a condition that if we were to stay together and get married, we'd go and live in the Middle East. Now, I would have preferred Lebanon, smaller, more relaxed and most importantly where the Aysha family are, it's by the sea. I had a stronger connection with Babaa's[14] family. Moving to Egypt wasn't a second option, it was the only option. Palestine was out of the question for us, and Nagwa[15] had been getting sick and needed more help, especially as 3'mad[16] was working out in T'gamma

---

14   Babaa – the name I call my father in law Dr Merhi Ayche. A wonderfully kind, gentle and generous man. Also the word for dad and father.

15   Nagwa – my mother in law

16   3'mad – pronounce Emad, my brother in law

khaimis in the university and she had a spare apartment we could move into, giving us time to find our feet and figure out where we wanted to live and get established.

It didn't take us long to narrow down where we wanted to live. I didn't want to move away from the Nile. Walking along that every day, I mean come on, it's the longest river in the world, measuring 4,135 miles or 6,650 km long... and for a water baby stuck in the middle of Cairo, that was a big deal. Being close to the ring road was also important as we didn't have a car. Getting the metro, flagging down a taxi or an auto bus was going to be easier. It also meant we could get to the different areas quicker... even if it still took on average an hour to go almost anywhere, and that is with steady traffic.

One thing I had understood 15 years previously upon my first visit to Cairo was that there was going to be traffic. Relentless traffic. ramO and I soon took to walking and using the metro pretty much everywhere we went, well unless of course we were not going to the centre. For a city the size of Cairo, there really should be an extra 10 main artery lines of metro track, and that is without serving the areas between the artery lines.

It was also a heck of a lot cheaper and I learnt so much about the culture watching people, interacting with the other ladies in the women-only carriages. I practised my Arabic with them, we laughed together and we discussed many subjects from children and motherhood, to the state of affairs, work and food. Food was always a favourite subject. Total random strangers just connecting on a metro, probably never going to see each other again, but you connect and talk like old friends. There were, of course, massive changes ahead that would see an end to this kind of interaction, and whilst I was there, I never saw it return.

Most of the time I would be looking out of the window whilst on the tram or taxi. I spent a lot of time just looking at the surrounding areas. The amount of shoe shops really surprised me when I first started travelling to Egypt, but now they had shops for absolutely anything. You could even have everything delivered. I am not joking, ANYTHING! I could get up and most of the shops would be open, go to bed and the shops would still be open. Egyptians work long hours. Drive long hours, and they do it in some of the toughest conditions. My respect for Egyptians was growing rapidly. I felt like a proper lightweight, totally overwhelmed by the heat, the dust, the noise and pollution.

The amount of homeless people shocked me the most, and the amount of young children on the streets was the worst for me. I knew that a lot of them were professional beggars for families and criminal gangs, that's the world over, but it was the ones that were 'lost'. The ones who had deep sorrow in their eyes. The ones who you could tell had lost everything, and everyone. Five and nine year old brothers sleeping in the grass verges in the middle of the directional lanes of traffic. The ones huddled together, sleeping on the steps of the metro stations. The family of five young brothers and sisters living in cardboard boxes and scavenging for food in the piles of rubbish, with international and national food chain restaurants and kushk owners close by, with their customers, wasting mountains of food, which could have very easily been given to these children.

I never understood the wastage in the UK from all the restaurants, supermarkets and high street shops, but to see starving children in amongst all these food places, looking for food in the piles of rubbish, I felt sick to my stomach. What kind of people were these? They had really tuned out. Become completely absorbed into the 'large crowd, no personal responsibility' mode. Because there were so many people, no one took action because of the 'someone else will do it' syndrome. But no one did.

I remember going to the grill house in Ma'adi, on shairah el silky[17] to get our dinner, and buying extra for the boys. Their little faces. With such surprise and gratitude. They were hungry. REALLY hungry. I have never seen a child so hungry to eat. I found myself holding back the tears. It wasn't even a lot, but they all shook my hand and said "shukrun" over and over again. A man from a nearby kushk told me off for feeding them and all I said was, "Ya haram," with the sadness in my heart. Here I was a mother of two boys of similar ages, getting grilled meats and salad for my boys and husband, seeing these five starving children, and I couldn't just walk on by. Due to the portion sizes in Cairo, and the fact that bread and rice come with pretty much every meal, there was too much for the boys and I. We would normally put it in the fridge and use it as we needed it, but this time I just bought extra meat and gave these boys all the spare rice and bread. It was a pleasure to see them eat and laugh.

I told ramO about it when I got home and he told me I couldn't keep

---

17   Shairah el silky – one of the main roads in Ma'adi Degla. Ma'adi Degla was on the outskirts of Cairo, heading out to Helwan, a much quieter area. One we looked at moving to.

doing it otherwise they will expect it and word would get around that I was doing it and then we would get followed by them and wouldn't be able to get rid of them. I remember thinking how heartless that was, not just about not feeding these five kids I had seen scavenging, but because I felt I had done something really lovely that he would be proud of me for and he just dismissed it.

For me, it was a difficult time. I had become so overwhelmed by everything I was seeing for the first time in my life, and I was 33. I was getting present to just how spoilt, expectant and pampered we are in the UK, Europe, the USA and all the other countries I had visited over the last 20 years. I didn't travel to countries and visit tourist areas either. I went 'local' every time. Learning about different cultures has always been a very keen interest of mine ever since I grew up. Living in a small village with an international farm camp had provided me with a mix of people from different countries exploring the world working. It gave me a hunger to see the world.

I found out over my three and a half years in Cairo that, like any city in the world, it is easy for people to go unregistered on government records. And with a lack of infrastructure within the country's administration offices, it was even easier than ever. I get that with computerising everything leaves governments open to hackers, other governments listening in (we only have to see the power of advertising and Facebook messenger scans prompting us to set an alarm or a diary entry if dates and times are mentioned), but the negative impact on the country as a whole was substantial; being one of the multitude of reasons why people chose to rise up against Mubarak. A movement I was fully behind. Things needed to change. The country was being raped, and the people along with it.

National schools, for example, are in such a state of disrepair that in the UK, we would have torn down the building (and probably built gardenless 'luxury apartments' and carparks, so I guess there is something to be said for keeping the school a school). One of these schools is the Gamal abdel Nassar school in Nasr City.

I remember being at a Ramadan charity event to feed 5,000 hungry people in 2011, held there, and being told it was one of the best government schools in Egypt. I thought it was a disused building that had been abandoned years ago; in parts not finished. There were the steel reinforcement rods that go inside concrete columns that were sticking out of the ground, the walls;

concrete stairways that had massive gaping holes in it going to the first floor classrooms. The biggest hole was big enough to fit a 20 stone adult through it, leaving children aged 7-11 ample space to fall through. The gardens were overgrown with broken and rusted metal remains of a slide or swing, part hidden, yet another danger to the children.

The school may have been broken but the spirit of the people gathered certainly wasn't. There was many 200 people of all ages, families with young children, youth groups, charities and student volunteers coming together to work outside and in small crowded classrooms, with no air conditioning, desks piled high in the corner of the classroom, with sacks of lentils, black eye beans, rice, oil, salt, sugar, along with several other items being loaded into boxes ready to distribute to those in the community who had nothing.

This is the most beautiful thing about the Egyptians, they have a steely resilience to life. Very similar to the Lebanese, especially those in the south, who've rebuilt themselves over and over again. There is a strength that resonates all around. You feel it, but can't describe it. It's a mindset of 'just keep going'. To be able to work as hard as the Egyptians do in the heat, and the amount of people – overrun with tourists, which simply adds to the vast amount of people already living there – gives an intensity that makes you shift. You have to just keep to the pace.

Getting on a metro once in Giza, my first trip out alone, I stood waiting for the older ladies and women with children to get on first. The next thing I knew a ladies arm came out of the carriage and pulled me on. When I was on she smiled at me and said, "You're not in England now." To which I had to laugh. It was just one of the many moments of connecting with people. She and I talked for the rest of our journeys and yet again, I gained a simple understanding of how to get along in a city this big.

Going back to the school situation, I was beginning to understand the structure. You see, in Egypt you have several layers to society. It has a really divided class system, which is so in your face, and yet goes against many teachings in the Qur'raan, about equality. This was highlighted during a meeting I attended with a driven young man called Ibrahim Saker. He was working on a project to start up JCI Egypt, and already had three others on a team. Ibrahim explained to me about the challenges they were facing to get licensed to set it up, and asked me to come along as I had been an active member of JCI back home in the UK.

Being Patrons Director of one region and a Patron of another region, or chapters as they were known, gave me insights from all perspectives of what kind of people they needed to be networking with to build a paying membership and team of invested patrons.

During the meeting I was asked to do a 10 minute presentation on what JCI was like back in the UK. When I asked them about the kind of members they were going for and how they were marketing, they had some pretty good ideas, but they had missed a fundamental point. JCI was for everyone who wanted to get involved in their community, develop life skills which positively impact all areas of your life and the life of others, either through social, business or community events, locally, nationally and internationally.

When I asked them what they would do if a young man in a gallebeya walked in and wanted to join, they all laughed and the guy acting as President said, "I'd ask him if he'd got lost!" then continued to laugh.

I found this arrogance distasteful. Everyone should be given the chance to make a difference. If they have the hunger and the drive to make something of themselves and their community, then they are the perfect members. But the team in place were more interested in feeding their own egos and excluding others they didn't feel met their exacting standards and levels of prestige. Potential members were asked to send CVs, go through an interview system and were judged on the amount of money they appeared to have, the kind of school they went to, who their families were and who they currently worked for.

To judge a person on the performance of their parents, and the current place of employment, when you are joining an international volunteer organisation that offers you training and support to grow and prosper, whilst enabling your community, country and world to prosper, showed a lack of understanding of personal growth, completely the wrong attitude and far too much ego. When I explained all this to them, in the nicest possible way of course, the room fell silent – especially, as I explained, that everyone in the room was a Muslim and if they truly believed in the teachings and the example of the Prophet Mohammed, they wouldn't be thinking or behaving in this way. This comment didn't go down very well, and to be honest I wasn't really bothered. I knew after this meeting that if the acting president and his two sidekicks were going to remain, I was staying as far away from it as possible.

After the meeting, a guy called Mahmoud came up to me and introduced himself. He wanted to learn more about JCI and about the work I had done previously. He also invited me to go along for coffee with a few of the others that were in the meeting. So off we went to Costa just around the corner, and little did I know at that point, I had found a new chosen little brother. Mahmoud is an incredible soul. He has so much passion and drive to help others. He is a totally selfless, hugely generous and incredibly humble.

That night whilst we chatted about JCI, his questions, understanding and ideas just kept shouting President at me. So, I asked him why he hadn't run for JCI President. He was surprised by my question and so were a few others. When I explained to him that he was the perfect president to lead JCI Egypt, he started to giggle and shake his head (and as I type this a HUGE smile has spread across my face, because I have seen this look on his face a thousand times – because he knows I call him on his bullshit and challenge him to step into who he really is – and he knows there is no escape!).

We all stayed and discussed JCI, the state of Egypt, how the energy was changing and how things needed to change, life, Islaam and a whole host of random subjects. I hadn't laughed or discussed business or personal development, coupled with politics and enjoyed it so much ever before. As I got up to leave, numbers were exchanged, goodbyes said and then Mahmoud surprised me by insisting he would accompany me back to Ma'adi before heading home to Sho'bra, adding at least an extra couple of hours to his day.

When I finally relented and accepted his offer, we continued talking about the prospect of him taking over as President. How ironic when I think back to this conversation now, especially as we were about to see the over-throwing of Mubarak and then a full-on, blood-thirsty military coup.

During the next month, Ibrahim and I met up to discuss the future of JCI in Egypt, the struggles they had been having growing it and how they could overcome the competition of AISEC. We met up in private gardens along the Nile, a place ramO and I would take the boys. It had a nice park, decent café/restaurant and a wonderful breeze that cooled you whilst you sat overlooking the lush grass on the other side of the Nile. Whilst sitting here in this garden, I would read, look up, take in my surroundings and breathe deeply. Here I was, a farmer's daughter from Friday Bridge, a mono-cultural area, which doesn't like outsiders – including the Londoners – sat less than a half-mile from my new home, looking out over the Nile. This was my new back garden, and I loved it!

Things were progressing really well in pretty much every area of life, I was making contacts, had stayed in touch with Mahmoud and Ibrahim with JCI, the boys were doing well at school, and I was getting the first draft of my manuscript for *Friday Bridge* written.

I had been put in touch with a friend of a friend and we had arranged to meet up for coffee with other ladies, many who were also integrated ex-pats. I couldn't think of anything worse than being surrounded by your typical ex-pats. People living in a country and not integrating? Not my bag. In my opinion not only do you integrate, you learn the language, the subtleties of the culture and you learn to cook the food. I was looking forward to meeting all these women. I needed some female company, and apparently one of them owned a book shop! How excited was I?!

The only area of my life that wasn't working was me being dependent on ramO. My Arabic was good, but it was nowhere near good enough to keep up with the quick pace the locals spoke at, known across the Arabic speaking world as 3ameyya[18]. And with my Arabic being a mix of Egyptian, or Misri, Shaami[19] and Gulf Arabic – not to mention many of the traditional words of old and Qur'raanic Arabic, with a dusting of Modern Standard Arabic thrown in for good measure – I knew I had to take lessons.

I also knew I had to do what I love doing — working! I had to make some money. There were too many things I wanted to do here in Egypt and I have never been one to ask for handouts, even from my husband. My mother used to call me an independent little madam, and yep! Totally own that mother – thank you! xx

I also knew ramO was still dealing with all the bureaucracy of getting all the paperwork sorted. Nearly four months in and it still wasn't sorted due to an incredible amount of incompetence and lack of communication across government offices. He was also looking for work and dealing with his mother; the latter being a task in itself.

It is no secret that this woman and I didn't like each other. Having told me on my wedding day ramO was marrying the wrong sister, she had never liked the idea that I stood up for myself, although she fought with everyone for her rights, and what she thought were her rights. The ironic thing is, I admire

---

18   3ameyya – means colloquial and is pronounced am-may-ya

19   Shaami – Arabic from Palestine, Syria, Lebanon and Jordan – a region in the Middle East. Pronounced Share-me

her. She has a pair of balls bigger than most men I meet in Egypt. She will fight to the death to protect what is hers. She has achieved much in her years and done so as a strong woman in a man's world, and in Egypt. It is hard enough working in an all-male environment in the UK, let alone in Egypt, and through the decades she has done it. I respected her, and I learnt a lot from her. Whether she likes to admit it, I know she learnt a lot from me, and I know that pissed her off. There were moments when I would come back at her with a one-liner, or a comment in a conversation with family, that would make her laugh, and then she would look at me with a kind smile, a nod and a wink. These are the moments I like to remember about her, because these are the moments when she was relaxed and at peace in the moment. She is an incredibly stunning woman when she allows the anger to leave her. But in the years I knew her, all 18 of them, I only saw this a handful of times.

The other challenge I had was with my mind. I felt like a burden. I had always been able to get stuff done, go places, create results and quickly; at the moment, I was not creating the results I wanted to see. Speak with others and they would be impressed with what I achieved in the first four months, but I had an issue with being kind to myself. I still hadn't made that mental shift to living and working in Egypt. ramO was also getting frustrated with the amount of questions, explanations and tasks expected of him, and who can blame him? In the 12 years we had been married, I had been self-sufficient, raised the boys pretty much single-handedly, whilst running the business and keeping on top of the home decorating and finances. He had travelled extensively with our business, something I encouraged him to do; especially after he got his UK passport and wasn't checked against the 'black list' for inappropriate activities due to his Palestinian refugee document. Seeing him able to travel freely with the UK passport gave me joy, because it gave him joy. The world was now his oyster and being a globally-minded couple, it simply made sense that we travel. ramO working abroad meant the boys and I also got to travel regularly.

For ramO, shifting into the full-time husband and father was a challenge, moving back to Egypt was a challenge, but I know the hardest one for him was speaking Arabic. Having not spoken it very much since he left Egypt, he was rusty in his Arabic. He looked Egyptian, was Egyptian but his Arabic was broken and gave him a lack of confidence that made him uncomfortable. We were both the same in that respect. We weren't patient with ourselves.

We both had to learn to be kind to ourselves, like we were with others.

We also had to re-learn how to live together, parent together and work together, instead of just two individuals that loved one another and had children together, and lived together. Teamwork in close quarters was very different to teamwork across countries and the phone. It took me a while to get used to him disciplining the boys. I had been their main care giver, the only parent other than at weekends every two to three weeks. I wasn't used to anyone else getting involved with their upbringing. There would be moments when we disagreed with the course of action taken, I was too soft, did, or explained too much. He was too harsh, and too lenient and didn't explain enough. It was a new balancing act we had to master together, but we would do it. We'd been through so much together already that this wasn't going to be an issue.

The tipping points

The day had arrived that I was going to meet with a woman called Sigrun. I had been told she was from Iceland, was married to an Egyptian named Omar and had two children; a boy between the ages of Khaalid and Naasir, and a daughter. We had arranged to meet up at her home and she would introduce me to other women who came along to the halaqa[20].

I missed my friends Ali, Debbie and Amira so much since I had arrived. We used to get together weekly for coffee and cake and to have not seen them for almost five months had been hard. I had always kept friends at a distance, never really letting anyone in, until I met these three beautiful women. If it hadn't been for Debbie, you wouldn't be reading this book now. She has saved me in more ways than one, and I don't think I will ever be able to express how much I love this woman. (Yes Debbie Miller!! YOU!)

Before I arrived I was really anxious. I hadn't spent time with a group of women on a personal level for a long time, or made any new friends. I'd made acquaintances, but not really friends for quite a few years. Mahmoud and I were still at a level of business and colleagues, but I knew that if I was to survive Egypt, and thrive as I wanted to, I needed some like-minded female friends who got 'it'; friends that got me; got being a mother and a business woman.

I arrived at Sigrun's and I nearly didn't knock on the door. Nearly turned around and went back home again; instead I sat on the steps of the stairway of the building and regrouped. I told myself that this was no different to

20   Halaqa – a regular meeting of minds to discuss Islaam

meeting someone in a shop and connecting. It was no different to going to a business networking meeting and meeting new people, except I hadn't done that in a couple of years due to the life threatening complications with my second pregnancy with Naasir.

I was about to call ramO, but something stopped me. I didn't feel I could bother him with this. I needed to do this by myself, as I had become accustomed to. He would only get irritable with me anyway, as he had enough to deal with, so I took a deep breath, told myself I could do it and knocked on the door. Hearing a friendly voice ask through the door who it was, and then for the door to be opened, with a big friendly smile there to greet me was reassuring. I went in, said hi to everyone and chose to sit nearest the window looking out over the Nile. It helped give me the space I needed to breathe and deal with the claustrophobic feeling I now got in new groups of people. I had never been this bad before. I always got nervous meeting new people, wondering whether they would like me, or not.

But now, I worried about pretty much everything. Was I too smart, or not smart enough? Was I too well informed and too political, too opinionated, too direct, too this or too that. My self confidence that had grown over the years was now disappearing and I didn't know why. I knew I had to dig deep and find out why I was like this.

There were several ladies already at Sigrun's and they all seemed very lovely; I knew almost immediately from listening to what they were saying that I wasn't the only opinionated woman with a brain in the room. Another wave of relief came over me. The introductions were made, along with juices and cups of tea.

I sat next to an Australian woman called Rowaida. I loved the energy she radiated, her big smile and the things she was saying. I kept my eye on her, I knew instantly if I was going to make friends with anyone in this room it was going to be her. More people came and I got to speak with Sigrun more, we had a LOT in common and I liked her.

After an hour of chatting, drinking juices, the food started to come out of the kitchen. I gave Sigrun a hand and so did Rowaida whilst the other ladies were discussing the chosen verse of the Qur'raan for that week. I listened carefully to what they had to say and found myself disagreeing with pretty much everything they said. The more they spoke, the more I disagreed, but I kept quiet and just simply listened.

Then the conversation turned to schools in Cairo and which ones were the better ones to go to for Islaamic knowledge, ex-pat integration and a whole host of other credentials to measure a school by. I listened very carefully to this because I had already decided I didn't want the boys to carry on going to Sahara International School. It was a two hour bus ride every morning and every night for the boys, and I hated the thought of my boys on a bus, without me in the Cairo traffic. Yes it was a school bus. Yes it had a driver and a school matron, but I still hated the fact I wasn't doing the school run. My boys didn't run out of school into my arms each day, as I had become accustomed to with Khaalid and I didn't like how tired we all were due to the early rise and early to bed scenario unfolding. I like quality family time and this current schooling set up wasn't working for me.

Due to the nature of the narrative the ladies were sharing about the schools, I knew I wanted to keep away from schools such as Amgad which had a salaafi, very conservative slant on the education.

I also knew I wanted to stay away from Islaamic schools full stop. If anyone was going to teach my boys about religion and their spirituality it was going to be me. I wanted them to have an open mind, for them to make their own choices about their faith, if they chose to have one. It was one of the reasons I chose Arabic names rather than Islaamic names.

I chose to really get involved in this discussion because it was really important to me to find a good school locally and one that had a mix of nationalities. Some of the schools I had enquired about were far too elitist for my liking, and more expensive than the private school they had attended in the UK. I didn't want my boys to go to a school where looking down on others simply because they didn't have as much money was acceptable. I had met quite a few parents from some of these elite schools, spoken with members of the administration team and my energy just went haywire and told me to avoid them like the plague. Others were just too far away.

Getting my head around the schooling system took a while, because in the UK we have private and state schooling. Yes, some of these have a religious leaning to them, but private and state is pretty much the way things are done. In Egypt however, it is a whole different ball game. How I am about to describe these schools doesn't sit well with me, but to get the point across and the subtleties, I am going to have to describe them this way.

So, the first level of schooling in Egypt is the government schools, such as the one mentioned earlier – the Gamal abdel Nassar in Nasr city. This is the free schooling in Egypt. This is where children go whose parents either do not work, are ba'waabs or farmers. The lower class people who live very humble lives and live off the land, and if you ask me, some of the nicest people I met in Egypt.

The next level of schooling is the National schools. These are for the first level of paid for schooling and they vary drastically. English is spoken in a lot of national schools as a second language, and sometimes not at all. The buildings are in a better state of repair than the government schools but not by much. Some of the school buildings look like abandoned or condemned buildings, well to me they do, having grown up in the UK. These schools will cost anything up to 11,000LE (£1,100) and when you consider the national average wage in Egypt is 100LE (£10) a month, you can see the level of society that goes to the national schools.

You then have the International Schools. This is where the biggest fracture in the schooling system happens. Some of the National schools have added the primary years as an International schooling programme using the CIPP – Cambridge International Primary Programme, not to deliver the higher standards of education you understand; just so they could charge more and have more prestige. These schools charge anything from 12,000LE (£1,200) up to 30,000LE (£3,000). The level of teaching didn't improve, nor did the buildings. Some of the books improved (with the sample and welcome packs being the bulk of the library, but the parents were being ripped off BIG time. I had a real issue with Cambridge University for not having better checks on this schools that ran their CIPP systems, because to me they were part of the corruption and deceit that the owners of these schools were part of. My argument is simply this, if someone uses your logo to promote their business, and you are aware that they are using your logo, then you have a duty of care to make sure that the product or service being delivered measures up, otherwise you take action to either increase training, performance or you ensure the organisation doesn't use your logo – and make it publicly known. It is called integrity.

The next level of schooling is where you have the education delivered entirely in English and with cross curricular learning from a range of resources. These schools tend to have both the National and the International school in the same school, and yet the two schools (National and International) are not allowed to mix with each other (and it is not due to numbers in the playground either). These schools charge anything from 18,000LE (£1,800) up to about 70,000LE (£7,000).

The next level of schooling is the top of the food chain and offer only American, British, German or French schooling. There is not a National school anywhere to be seen and these schools are all brand new, purpose built schools. These will cost you in the region of 70,000LE (£7000) minimum, and anywhere up to 250,000LE (£25,000).

Now these figures may not seem a lot to some of you, but when you consider these prices are the entry level prices for your five year old, and will only increase with each year group they progress in; then you consider that many families have three and four children, you start to really see a divide in the overall society. These costs again are all without any supplies, uniforms or school trips. You will still be given a list of supplies to provide your child with so they can do the work in class.

Hearing all of this broken down over a bite to eat on my first meeting with fellow mums was mind blowing. Hearing some of the things on the supplies list was so shocking it was laughable. I just couldn't understand where the money was going. Then I was told that the schools with the least amount of supplies on the list were owned by non-Egyptians, and depending on whether the owner of the school was Egyptian or not would also depend on whether the school had a well-stocked library, whether the teaching staff of international origin would stay longer than the first open evening where parents were invited, and whether the school would simply be shut for the day.

Narrowing it down to location and excluding the Islaamic and national schools, we weren't left with many options, but the two schools I had chosen to speak with ramO about were only a 10 minute taxi ride away each day, meaning I could go with them in the morning and walk back after I had dropped them off. The taxi's wouldn't cost any more than the bus we had been paying for and it meant that the boys had more time to relax, play and do any homework. After much discussion with each other, and with more mums at more of Sigrun's gatherings, we chose Ma'adi Narmer School, or MNS as it was shortened to.

Meeting the ladies at Sigrun's was a life saver. Rowaida, Sigrun and another two ladies called Gitanjeli and Aziza were to become good friends of mine. We spent a lot of time in each other's company, and as we were all from different countries it felt a lot like life in the UK with my girlfriends there who came from a multitude of different nations.

Our friendships grew very quickly and we discussed everything and anything under the sun from parenting, cross cultural families and the challenges, food, Islaam and the media, books, Egypt and it's many challenges and how to survive it, and the sense that the air was changing; an energy shift. We also discussed the way in which Egypt had changed over the years, the attitudes, the men and the way in which harassment was getting worse all the time and how something in the country had to give. Something had to be done. Egypt just couldn't carry on with the way things were going as so many were wanting to leave; people who had vowed never to leave were now wanting to leave. There was to be another 'brain drain' soon, and with so many talented Egyptians leaving the country so they could thrive, commerce, science and IT didn't look good. I enjoyed these conversations, proper conversations about deeper stuff; and it was great that I had met a group of ladies so like myself in many ways. Making friends with them made me feel at home, and they even recommended another lady to me who would help us find our own place. I had had enough of living in my mother-in-law's apartment. She had too much say over how we lived, not to mention the décor and area were proving too much for me to deal with. So many confused patterns thrown together with a large helping of Louis XVI gold furniture everywhere, and the constant lack of sleep due to living next to the beladi area and their incessant use of guns during the night, did not make for a happy Dawn. Quite the opposite in fact. I became irritable and snappy, and resentful of this gift of an apartment to live in. I am a really grateful person, and it didn't sit well with me to offend the giver of a gift by refusing it; but I had to move out because in the first year of being in Egypt, living in this apartment, I didn't get one good night's sleep. I found myself falling asleep during the day, when I should have been working on building a life in Egypt. I was about to start writing my first book, I wanted to learn the language on a deeper level and I wanted to do something productive with my time, not catch up on sleep just because of some selfish idiots who thought firing guns into the air during the night was a fun thing to do. I kept imagining a bullet ricocheting off the building and hitting someone, or going through a bedroom window and killing a child; but cause and effect were obviously not part of the mindset of these people.

I remember one night ramO shouting down to them telling to pack it in, kids were sleeping and stop being so selfish. The gunfire stopped for the rest of the night, but I lay there in fear that they were going to fire in our direction and possibly get worse. Then I remembered a phrase I'd heard a little while before "Worrying is just praying for bad stuff to happen", so I took some deep breaths, did some meditation and went to sleep. Tomorrow was a new day.

One of the confronting things about moving to Egypt was the realisation of how spoilt we are in the UK. During one of our first days in Egypt I remember getting annoyed about how I was going to recycle and compost everything. Such a middle class European problem! Travelling about you realise that the 'state of the roads' back in the UK were nothing compared to the roads in Egypt; and pavements! Oh what a joy they are in the UK! If you find a pavement in Egypt that you are able to walk along, without dodging all the cars parked on them, then be happy. Most of the pavements in Egypt are either pop up car parks, broken or covered in rubbish…. Or a heaving human snake winding its way through the streets – well it is the fourth largest city in the world!

Power cuts are so common in Egypt that having a stash of candles and a lighter handy is a necessity. They kept you fit as well, especially as you would need to climb up several flights of stairs, dodging the rubbish scattered across the steps, which had been left out by neighbours, and been rummaged through by cats. In our first apartment building that would mean 16 very dark stairways to climb, even in the daylight. In our second apartment building it was only seven. There was a very big part of me that wanted to run up them each day to see how far and fast I could get each time I did it, but with the amount of food waste, the odd dirty nappy and heavens knows what on the stairways, it just wasn't something I ended up doing. The worrying thing for me here was that these apartments weren't low class apartments, where you could half expect to see this. These were the middle classes, the ones that could afford to send their children to the higher level national and International schools.

Litter is a massive problem in Egypt, and very few people actually care enough to do anything about it. There is a group called "Keep Egypt Clean", my argument with this was it needed to be clean first, like it had been some 10 years before. Egypt had gone through a massive clean-up, rubbish was removed, more bins were put out and it lifted the mood. I was hopeful that it would continue, but the pessimism friends and family spoke of back then, and had, was saddening. Here you have a nation of people who believe that the earth is a trust given to us by Allah, something to treasure and take care of, and they simply throw rubbish on the floor, leave it outside their apartments, not taking care to keep safe from cats. I hate litter. To drop litter is a selfish act, an act of disrespect to others, and you. It is an ignorant mindset, one of expectance that 'someone else will pick it up for me' and 'it's not my problem'. A mindset that is everywhere, not just in Egypt. In Egypt, I could understand it to some degree as there are no refuse collections, there are no 'dump it sites' or recycling centres like we have here in the UK and across Europe. The powers that be in Egypt only think of themselves and how they can rape the system and the people for their own gain. Why would they want to waste money on collecting litter when they could put it towards their son's multi-million pound apartment in London's Kings Cross? Well they wouldn't, would they?

Being able to have the windows and doors open during the day was something I missed, and I realised how much positive energy flows through the home when the windows and doors are open. Yes we could open the doors and pull the sheesh[21] across to prevent the flies and mosquitoes from coming into the apartment, but it didn't stop the sand or the dust from coming in. Five minutes with the doors open, with the sheesh closed, would bring in more dust than a week or two of leaving the doors fully open in England; and that is if there is not a sand storm.

The first sandstorm we witnessed was from the boys bedroom window in the first apartment we lived in. 16 floors up and we would see it rising, then swirling and then we could see nothing. A total blanket of sand and dust, with zero visibility; and the noise! Hearing all those tiny grains of sand, with the odd stone caught up in the mix, was quite scary to be honest. Like one of those scary spooky noises in a horror movie (please bear in mind I don't do horror movies!).

One of the 'horrors' of living in Egypt was being reminded of who was in charge EVERYWHERE you went. You couldn't travel 500m without seeing a picture of Mubarak. A reminder that his eyes and ears were everywhere;

---

21   Sheesh – a screen of mesh that prevents flies and mosquitoes from coming into your home.

whether it was with his secret police (who are not that secret), the beltagi[22] (often employed by the police in Egypt) or 'off duty' military that if they didn't like what you were talking about, or behaving then you would either disappear or be beaten to death like Khaalid Saeed, the young man beaten to death by Egyptian secret police, which helped incite the Uprising that was just around the corner. Seeing Mubarak's face everywhere was, I felt, insulting to the intelligence of the people. Here he was in all his arrogance, his smug face reminding the people of Egypt that he was in control, and should be feared; mocking them all whilst he raped his own country and that of the people. Walking along the corniche in Ma'adi photos were on both sides of the road, and the more I saw them, the more I wanted to slap him across the face. I'd been studying Egyptian and Arab politics for the best part of 15 years, travelled every year to see family there, as well as travelled across the rest of the Arab world. I went deep into the politics of the people, not just the politicians, but the people. I studied Arabic history going back over 2000 years. I understood the politics, the Islaamic religion and faith, and my heart ached for Egypt.

---

22   Baltagi – a thug, thuggery

Going down in history....
Egyptian Style.

The first time I had travelled to Egypt was in July 1999, the year I married ramO. A lot had changed since this visit. I had seen many things that blew my mind. Having only travelled to Europe I was not ready for the crazy sights and lifestyle that Egypt had to offer.

Coming out of the airport and seeing a whole family on a 'nifty fifty'[23] motorbike, and I literally mean a whole family – Both parents, one child sat on the handle bars, one between the parents, another hanging on for dear life at the back, and for those families with that one extra child, the mother would have them sat on one of her legs, holding onto them with her free arm, or the one not holding the shopping, was a familiar sight. It was a good job Egyptian traffic didn't move very fast! This is one of the things that never changed about Egypt, and almost felt like a homecoming gift. You knew you were in Egypt when you saw this. I never saw it in Lebanon, nor any of the other Arabic countries I visited.

I had learnt very basic Arabic and knew certain areas of Cairo, Fagala being one of them as my mother in law lived there. I knew Garden City quite well as the falucca's were there, along with the Cairo Museum in Tahrir square, just behind the line of hotels along the corniche.

I had learnt early on to either ignore or say "la shukrun!²⁴" to those in

---

23   Nifty fifty – a 50cc motorbike

24   La shukrun – no thank you

Khan el Khalili[25] selling their wares and inviting us to eat in their restaurants.

Having not been back to Egypt in a few years, I was slightly taken aback at the state of the streets. They had not only regained the little that had been cleared up years ago, but were now worse than ever. Why were the people not doing something about the state of their country? Why had they stopped using the communal gardens? Why had the lively, energetic conversations in the ahwa[26]'s quietened down? Why was the country falling apart around us? Even though I knew the answers to these questions, I still couldn't fathom why the people were just allowing it all to happen. Did they not love their country? Did they not actually get the scriptures in their holy books, telling them to fear no one but Allah, God or G-d? More importantly did they not love themselves and their children enough to rise up and say enough is enough?

I understood the fact that Egypt had been under martial law, since 1967, and under a state of emergency since Anwar el Sadat was assassinated in 1981 (by, I believe Hosni Mubarak). Congregating in the communal gardens meant the people could discuss the problems and share ideas and rise up, and that was not allowed. Disrespect Mubarak? Question how things were done? I don't think so!

Organise and create community projects, how dare you?! Being human, enabling others and showing how things should be done, was placing shame on the government. Making them look bad; that was not going to happen on Mubarak's watch. Him and his military allies were making too much money and running the show for their own benefit to enable others to get in their way and show how things should be done for community and country, for the good of everyone. Working together to solve the problems of the country was something that was done well under cover. Many groups that had organised, had either had the leaders 'dealt with' never to be seen again, or the lesser groups, such as the ones who organised make shift soup kitchens on trellis tables in the poorer areas, were confronted by the police or military, with the food they had made tipped over on the floor, tables smashed and individuals beaten. Badly. A warning, if you like.

If you owned a building, as one of my friend's Samir did, and someone decided to set up a stall right outside your building leaving rubbish and debris

---

25   Khan el Khalili - Very famous, busy, traditional market place in Cairo

26   A7wa – local coffee shops, mainly frequented by men for shisha's and lengthy afternoon conversations

outside all over the streets, obstructing residents from entering or leaving the building, then don't expect any support from the police or local authorities. The stall holder would just throw some rashwa[27] in their direction and if you dare to question the police or representative, then expect a beating yourself; or lots of inconvenient moments from then on. Some would continue to harass you for a few weeks, others would harass you for months, years and even generations depending on what it was that went on between you and the area they were from. Bruise the ego or humiliate an Egyptian and it could turn into a turf war like no other. Now please do not misunderstand me, I am not saying all Egyptians are like this, far from it, many are incredibly beautiful people, but many can be incredibly spiteful and territorial. It is deeply ingrained into the psyche of the people due to the centuries of a nomadic lifestyle and tribalism. The tyranny the Egyptians have lived under for decades, both foreign and domestic has also contributed. During my time in Egypt, whether it has just been visiting over the last 18 years, or whether it was living there, I have mixed with such a vast diverse group of Egyptians, as well as met lots of Egyptians here in the UK. When you speak with the honest ones amongst them, they will agree with me regarding the problems in Egypt. Those that live in the UK, but deny all problems in Egypt, when you ask them why they don't move back if there are no problems, are always stuck for an answer because they know there are HUGE problems in Egypt, and they don't want to have to deal with it. They want to bury their head in the sand and deny their home country has got to such a bad situation that they could never go back. An example of how Egyptians live in denial about the problems facing the country is the issue of Garbage City: a city where the people living there are living in piles and piles of litter, as high up as the fifth floor of apartment buildings. The people there live off the money they make from the recycling of materials, and the things they make. Many of the people who live there are incredibly poor and some actually live in the rubbish and scavenge in the rubbish piles for food to eat. However, if you ever ask an Egyptian "so what's this about Garbage City?" they will deny its very existence, but you know they know about it. You can't not know about it living in Egypt. When an article was written about Garbage City some years ago and featured in the Daily Mail newspaper and online, the fierce denial from the Egyptians was astounding. The nastiness and the venom displayed

27   Rashwa – money – a bribe

quite clearly showed the anger of Egyptians, even though it is something they allowed to happen, and they were embarrassed globally. Egypt is known as 'Um Dunnya[28]' and to embarrass Egypt was not acceptable on any level.

The ignorance, and the denial, along with the corruption are just some of the reasons so many leave as soon as they can, and why many more are working towards being able to leave. Egypt has suffered from quite a few brain drains over the last three decades, and whilst military rule is still in place, the more brain drains will continue. Egypt is ruled by the military, plain and simply; and it will continue to be for the foreseeable future because of the money and power the military have.

ramO and I considered looking for some land and building our own apartment building, but speaking with friends and family members who had tried, or were in the process of doing so, we both agreed that there was no way we were going to deal with the amount of problems these guys were talking of. ramO and I are up for a challenge, and we know there are problems with any new build, but the problems were simply in the process, just to be a problem. Another way for a government official to give themselves an ego boost, or a desperate attempt to feel important and have some control. If you wanted to build your own home, or set up a business, it would take years to simply sort out the paperwork before you could start. Friends of ours have been fighting to get their own home built for over 10 years now.

Others have been ripped off in the £10,000's due to a lack of integrity, honesty and let's be honest, a true belief in Allah that they proclaim to believe in; it wasn't those that were destitute that were stealing, it was the ones that had money, that had a source of income. I wouldn't blame the person who was homeless and hadn't eaten for stealing, but the arrogance of the men that rocked up in the 4x4, large selection of keys (just to show his importance) and his matching HUGE watch face all blinged out (just to show how wealthy he is), well to steal in his position, disgraceful! The worst thing about the 'practising' Muslims in Egypt, many had got to the point that prayer, or attending the mosque was done either out of habit or to show how religious and pious they were, to only go and steal, harass and goodness knows what else five minutes later.

The harassment had gotten really bad. I actually felt afraid this time in Egypt. I had walked alone in Egypt to the shops in Fagala a few times and

---

28   Um Dunnya – mother of the world

only experienced the Arab fascination of staring at anyone who looked remotely different. This time however, the harassment was a whole new level of sinister. Cars would follow me, and at first I thought they were asking for directions. Being used to giving directions in England, I didn't think anything of it at first, but as soon as I would stop to assist, I was met with the men touching their private areas, rubbing them up and down and licking their lips calling me "mozza[29]" or "aby'yad[30]".

I had young boys, and I mean young boys shout out to me, "I want to fuck you white lady," and what was scary, was some of them said it in English as well as in Arabic. One young boy, maybe aged 14 unzipped his trousers and pulled his penis out and started to masturbate right there in front of me whilst licking his lips and repeating, "mozza, mozza, mozza." 14!!! I mean seriously?? In a country as conservative and religious as Egypt, how does this happen. He was really quite shocked when I shouted "a3'iib[31]! Wa haram fi Islaam[32]!!"

One day whilst walking with my boys to the train station in Ma'adi, aged 10 and 6 at the time, on our way to 6th October to see Yasmine, I sensed someone following us. I scanned all the faces around us and noticed several guys staring at me and the boys through the windows of the doors that separated the men and the women's carriages. There were also a few guys who didn't care about the segregated carriages and were sat in the women's section staring at me and the boys. A couple of the older ladies shouted at the moment and told them to behave, and recited verses in the Qur'raan about how men should lower their gaze as a sign of respect to women, but these men just laughed in their faces. One older lady got so feisty with them, shouting at them, arms waving and a couple of the men dropped their gazes, their upper bodies and looked shamed. This woman then looked at me and the boys, nodded and said "hasib habibiti, hasib[33]", my response could only be "Elf Shuk ya tante, elf shuk[34]".

---

29 Mozza – sexy woman

30 Aby'yad – white, but used in this nature to 'compliment' a woman because the whiter you are the more attractive you are.

31 A3'iib – shame on your culture

32 Wa haram – and forbidden in Islaam

33 Hasib habibiti, hasib - Safely my beloved, safely

34 Elf shuk ya tante, elf shuk - 1000 thank yous Aunty, 1000 thank yous

The boys and I got off at Sadat, one of the main stations downtown and started walking towards the underground towards the metro that led us to Dokki, a location on the edge of Cairo inner city. As we got off the metro in Sadat, I had the sense of being followed again, so the boys and I circled around to try and lose whoever it was that was following us. I pretended to the boys, I just wanted to double check something. As I turned around I could see a man that I had seen in the men's carriage. He was just staring. Like REALLY staring. He had a sleazy look on his face and a grin that was making me feel very uncomfortable. I was not used to this kind of attention, not only because this had never happened to me in the UK, but also because I was really overweight and no supermodel. I was modestly dressed with my jeans and loose top on, with the headscarf tied in the African style, rather than the Arabic style. Nothing sexual, nothing that could have been enticing (and not that the way you dress should invite sleazy or inappropriate behaviour either!).

The boys and I made our way to the metro station and headed for Dokki, getting into the ladies carriage and walking all the way down the carriage to get lost amongst the women. I chose to stand with the women who had children, and whilst I was on the metro, I changed the way I had tied my scarf to see if I could lose this scumbag. Once off the metro, walking up the steps to meet up with Yasmine, all of a sudden I felt his presence behind me. He was standing so close behind me I could feel, and smell, his breath on the back of my neck. In his near perfect English, he told me that he was going to fuck me until I screamed for him to stop and he was going to do it with my boys watching. I froze. I didn't know what to do, but the fighter in me (and probably the foolish hot head in me) turned around and said "ragul mish nadiif kateer, a3'iib[35]!" And slapped him around the face, grabbed the boy's hands and ran across the road. I didn't even look for traffic, I just wanted to get away from this dirty, vile creature. A younger guy who stood nearby asked if I was okay, and I just looked at him. He repeated the question and I nodded and said, "Shukrun[36]"

The man had disappeared and, seconds later, Yasmine arrived. I put on a brave face because Yasmine worried about me travelling on the metro anyway, so this would have made her worry even more. I told her that a guy

---

35 Ragul mish nadiif kateer, a3'iib – you're a very dirty man, shame on your culture

36 Shukrun – thank you

had followed us but I never told her what he had said to me (so now you know Yasmine. I'm sorry I hid it from you habibiti[37] xx).

I found out not long after meeting Sigrun and Rowaida that there was now an actual app called Harass map, whereby women could pin on a map where they were harassed so a picture of the most uncomfortable and dangerous areas of Egypt were. The sad thing is about the harassment in Egypt, some women blame other women for being out of the house, which in their minds means you deserve to be harassed, men simply laugh it off as if it is not a problem and say, "Oh they are harmless! Don't worry about it!" But the thing is, it is a constant daily intrusion of your mental and emotional wellbeing, and it is also a physical thing. The amount of men that would grab your backside as you are walking by, that would grab your breasts and walk away laughing. Cairo has become a dirty place to visit in many guises and if this is what it is to live in the most religious of countries, then book me a ticket on the first plane out! I saw Muslims surrounding me everywhere, but saw very little Islaam. But my belief in organised religion was fading anyway. My faith was still as strong as it had always been. I still believed in a higher entity, an energy force, but religion…? The more I learnt about history, date, symbol and imagery transference, the more about socio-economics in the regions of the revelations, the more Arabic I understood, the deeper I went, the more I realised that you don't need religion to guide you, you just need morals and values, and they were in HUGE decline here in Egypt. I kept seeking knowledge and I don't think Sigrun knew what had hit her when I arrived at her book shop… talk about a child in a candy shop!!

Life in Egypt was unfolding nicely in many respects. We had started to make friends, many of which came over to the apartment on my birthday to help me celebrate. It was a good party, lots of introductions between old and new friends, all of which had children close in age to the boys. It was also a chance to learn more about stuff to do in Egypt. Ehab and Deena were really helpful and suggested loads of places that they knew both ramO and I would love. They had known ramO since being together at the AUC, and they had three children, roughly the same age as Khaalid and Naasir, so the house was full of children and adults having a great time. Aziza's little girl was absolutely smitten with Khaalid, and became his shadow every time we met up. Aziza was the complete opposite to me and was the biggest

---

37   Habibiti – my beloved (f)

"germophobe[38]" I'd ever met. How she managed to keep her sanity in Egypt was beyond me. She had some really great tips though on how to clean and keep things clean in Egypt, many of which were sanity saving!

The boys and I were learning more Arabic, school was still an issue because much of the work sent home for the boys to do was not correct. There was a lot of going back and forth between the school and I because the teaching staff were asking me to correct what I thought was wrong. I asked them to put me on the payroll if that is what they wanted. That didn't go down very well and I got a lecture from them on how we must work together for the good of our children, and how it is our religious duty to contribute positively. I was so close to removing the boys from school and home schooling them but events soon took over whereby them continuing to go to school was no longer an option anyway.

I started making a timeline and set deadlines to write my book, and yet I was still looking for an editor, and a publishing house. I had the funding in place, so I just started writing it. Everything would fall into place. It was an interesting process writing my first book, wondering if anyone will buy it. I mean come on, who am I? I'm not famous, I am just me. Yet after some promotional activities, I already had two interviews lined up for other people's books to be published in the States, as well as the one in the UK, and people were already telling me they couldn't wait to read my book. I kept thinking, "Why do so many people, who I do not know, follow my blog and my articles?" I just couldn't get it. It was an interesting process of owning who I am and believing I had a contribution to make to the world. I guess part of me, didn't want me to get it because I wasn't ready to be able to own it; and I kept telling myself "maybe it's a good job I don't see in myself what others see, I'll become arrogant or scared, and neither of those are endearing or useful to my soul. So I just started writing. Writing until I couldn't write any more. Many of my paragraphs morphed into articles for my blog rather than my book, but that was cool, it was building an audience ready for when my book came out.

I started making lists of possible options. I considered continuing my teaching of English and English Literature privately, or in schools, but I was unsure of the logistics of that yet, especially given that I needed to devote my time to preparing a meal for when my children return home from school,

---

38   Germophobe – someone who sanitises frequently and excessively

and then help them with their home work! I was also keen to continue my radio appearances with the BBC, wondering how to transfer the radio appearances into actual live/recorded TV appearances; and as we also now had Press TV (which is great, by the way!) I added another outlet for my media appearances!

During the December 2010 school holidays, I remember planning to take the boys to the Cairo Museum in Tahrir square. I had been in touch with a new friend Flip who was a native American, married to an Egyptian, and we were planning to go together and make a day of it.

I remember being on the phone with her and we were talking about how the energy had changed. We knew there were going to be protests. We knew that people were getting really frustrated and angry. We also knew that people were done with the state of the country, not being able to progress under the suffocation of the oppressive regime, but both Flip's husband and ramO laughed at us for our "hippie views" on the energy change comments. We'd agreed to go down to Tahrir on the Tuesday, 25th January when she had got back from her travels, so I set about planning some activities for the boys, looking at what work they were doing in school and how we could combine that with the visit to the Museum. I even sat and watched Night at the Museum with them and created a quiz for them to complete whilst we were at the museum, a quiz they would never get to complete.

The straw that broke the camel's back.

I remember watching the TV and seeing the reports of the protests starting in Tunisia, or rather Tunis as I know it as. ramO and I were discussing whether Egyptians would rise up, whether they had it in them to finally take a stand against Mubarak. He was highly skeptical like most people were. He knew the Egyptian people better than I did as he'd lived there and could have more open conversations with people due to his Arabic language and ethnicity, as well as the fact that he was a man. There is a lot of sexism in Egypt, so when people in the UK talk about gender inequality and how unfair things are… it makes me laugh at the 'terrible' things they experience when, as my nan would say, "Kids today don't know they are born." I believed that the Egyptians had what it took, and reminded him about Ibrahim and Mahmoud who wanted to start JCI. I mentioned the Harass Map, Keep Egypt Clean groups, discussed conversations I'd had with my new friends, and how we believed that things were changing; people were getting angrier, more frustrated and more vocal about it. He still refused to believe anything would happen in Egypt. They were too scared of Mubarak to do anything, and if they were going to do something, they'd have done it years ago.

Watching the uprising in Tunis kick off across TV and social media, following the political public suicide of Mohammed Bouazizi, with film footage and photos of protests, people dying in large numbers due to the Tunisian Police, was both scary and exciting. I was scared because what I saw could very easily happen in Egypt, but with more people, deeper anger and frustrations, entwined with a more aggressive culture. I was excited because it meant the people were actually going to grow a backbone and stand up for themselves, and that meant a major shift in consciousness, hopefully a positive one. Both countries were at a point where the levels of unemployment, low wages, poor quality of life, high food prices, corruption, lack of political freedom when it came to freedom of speech had reached its pinnacle, and the people were finally finding their voices.

Seeing the President Zine El Abidine resign on the 14th January, some 28 days after the revolution started, gave great hope to the Egyptian people, and everyone was talking about it. You couldn't go into a shop, or café, or get together with your friends without it being discussed.

If the energy in Egypt had changed in December, then it certainly changed on the 14th January. It was as if there was a spark in the air. A tension building. An excitement. People questioning how the government had gone about blocking Wikileaks, shutting down certain websites, and even going to the extent of stealing people's passwords and removing private posts on their Facebook. People were in uproar about it. How could they do that? What right did they have to do that? Legally speaking, they had none. In a human rights setting, they certainly didn't have any rights to do it; but they did. And if they could do it, anyone could. Many people joked that Egypt was so fucked when it came to IT infrastructure internally within the government that there were no systems worthwhile hacking into, and with the uproar that had happened with Tunis, the Egyptian government surely wouldn't allow any protests to happen, let alone shut down the internet. But the more people discussed it, the more the fire in their bellies grew and on the morning of the 25th January, the very morning I was due to meet Flip at the Cairo Museum in Tahrir, that fire exploded onto the streets of Cairo and started one of the most historic moments in modern day history…. And here was I, with my boys, in Egypt to witness it; slightly more of an adventure than I had been wanting for the boys and I, but hey life has a way of surprising you, especially in Egypt.

It was about 10am that I turned on the TV under the orders of Flip who couldn't believe I hadn't heard the protests had started. I called to ramO and he came in to the lounge to look at the news. I told Flip I would call her back, I needed to speak with ramO.

Once off the phone, I sprung into action. I told ramO that the boys would obviously stay with me, as it made more sense for him to go down to the protests. If he thought the protests were safe enough, then the boys and I would make our way down there later that day. He looked at me and I simply said "Well you are going, aren't you? Don't think you are going to be one of those people that sits around moaning about a situation, and then not go and do anything about it!" He looked at me and laughed, not knowing whether I meant it or not. To which I responded, "You ARE GOING ramO. You have the chance to be part of history here, you've said for years Mubarak needs to go, and now there is an opportunity to add your voice to the movement in a positive way, and you think you are staying at home? I don't think so!" He had a grin on his face, and I couldn't quite tell if he was proud of me for attempting to kick him out of the door to stand up and be counted for something he believed in, or whether he was simply nervous about going. We both knew things were going to kick off BIG TIME, but just how big we didn't know.

For the next hour I kept asking him when he was going down. He kept telling me he was sorting it out. I wasn't having it. There was nothing to sort out, he was just procrastinating. I told him that if he didn't get his arse down into Tahrir, he could stay at home with the boys and I would go. One of us needed to be there because we always talked the talk, attended anti-war, pro-Palestine marches in the UK, and now it was time to walk the walk. He was getting really annoyed with me pressuring him into going, but I wasn't going to stop until he was out the door. As he was leaving, I told him I was proud of him, told him to keep himself safe and to let me know when he arrived in Tahrir. He said he would, gave the boys a really big hug, told them he loved them and what he was going to do, and that he would see them later. He gave me a really tight hug, told me he loved me and thanked me for getting on his case about going. I told him I would see him later and that I loved him. We then looked each other in the eyes, knowing that depending on what he encountered in Tahrir, it may be the last time we saw each other. He looked again to the boys and then back to me, when Naasir shouted out, "Family hug!!" Which is something we had lots of.

We piled onto the bed and had a big massive family hug, lots of tickles and laughter and then ramO said, "Right then, I'll text you when I get there," and with that he left the apartment.

The boys went back into their room and started playing with their lightsabers pretending to be Jedi's. I sat down and the reality of what had just happened hit me. I had just told my husband that he must go and protest, knowing what I had seen in Tunis, I had probably just sent my husband to his death. I stood up to go make a cup of tea, because like any English person knows, a cup of tea always steadies the nerves and solves everything. Whilst making the tea, the tears started to fall. What if I never saw him again? I started to go over everything we had been through with each other, and how much I loved this man. I thought of the stories I would tell the boys about him as they grew up. I thought of everything that he had wanted to achieve and how I would go about making them happen in his memory. I also went through a mental checklist of all the things I would need to do with regards to our lives logistically. There was no way I would stay in Egypt with his mother, so I started to make plans to either go live with Baaba in Oman, or travel home to the UK. Then I started giggling to myself. What the fuck was I doing? Putting out there into the universe that I would be a widow before the end of the day! Well that was NOT going to happen. ramO would be calling any moment and he would be coming home that night to a delicious meal, and lots of hugs from the boys and I.

Within five minutes of sorting my head out, the phone rang. It was ramO. He sounded so excited. He was meeting friends down in Tahrir and everyone was on their way. Literally everyone. He told me that the mood was one of excitement and people were talking and laughing with each other on the metro like he had never seen. There were fathers and sons together. Banners in people's hand, along with the Egyptian flag tied around their shoulders or on sticks in the hands of the children. Men, women, children, young and old all joining forces to get rid of Mubarak. I hadn't heard him sound so excited for such a long time. It was one the best phone calls I had ever had with him. At the end of the call he thanked me again, and told me he would see me later. I told him to just to let me know what his ETA would be and I'd finish cooking ready for his arrival home.

He called me a while later and told me that even though the mood had been jubilant on the metro, the closer he got to Tahrir the more the energy heightened and he could feel the anger. Some of those with children decided to turn back, others continued on. Things were hotting up and I had seen the events unfolding on Al Jazeera. It wasn't looking good. It was looking particularly dangerous actually. ramO reassured me he was cool, and was more positive now he was meeting up with others in Tahrir. He promised to phone me when he could and then said goodbye.

As soon as that call ended, I had many text messages ping into my inbox. Sigrun, Rowaida, Gitanjeli, Flip and another friend called Kirsty. I had messages from Mahmoud, Ibrahim all telling me what was happening near them and around them as Mahmoud and Ibrahim were down in Tahrir. I jumped straight onto Facebook and Twitter, connecting with people that Sigrun had recommended. I checked the status updates of other friends, and the photos and updates they were showing were of people in large numbers congregating at the metro stations, in Tahrir, roads full of people walking towards Tahrir. The photos showed faces full of joy. One friend posted, "Finally I get to see my fellow countrymen and women join together to reclaim our country."

Other status updates were ones of threats to Hosni Mubarak telling him to stand down, he wasn't wanted. Others were of family and friends back home tagging me in status updates wanting to know what was happening. Before I knew it, I was blogging every day on the events as they unfolded, updating friends and strangers on what was happening around me, as well as what was really going on in Egypt.

During each day, ramO would text me to let me know what was happening. He came home every night, showing me photos of what had been going on. The police brutality, the blockades, the fires being set in shops, all the fast food shops having their windows smashed due to the rocks and boulders being thrown at the police to stop them arresting people or beating them up. They didn't want people in Tahrir and they would stop at nothing to make sure the people were under control. But they couldn't control the numbers. In Tahrir, Giza, Alexandria, Suez, Tanta, Ismalaya and in every city and town, open space where people could protest they did. The posters of Mubarak, that lined the streets everywhere, we torn down or defaced and I couldn't have been happier!

During the afternoon on the 27th, Sigrun and Rowaida came over as all our husbands were in Tahrir and instead of being at home alone with the kids, we thought it would be a good idea to get together. There had been rumours that the government were going to shut down the internet, stop people tweeting photos and video footage, and sharing them on Facebook. The three of us were discussing it in the dining room, and checking our connections right by the router. We all had family and friends who were frantic with worry. What they were seeing on the BBC, Al Jazeera and other news channels were differing greatly. Al Jazeera as you can imagine didn't hold back. The BBC was more protective over the sensitivity of its audience. Russian and French TV news channels sat firmly in the middle of the two. Egyptian state TV, well according to them, there was nothing going on. No protests, no troubles and just more and more government rhetoric and lies. Sigrun tried to reply to a friend's message on Facebook to reassure them everything was okay, but the page wasn't loading. We all looked at each other and all of us at the same time had a grin of shock and disbelief on our faces, and all of us said at the same time "They haven't!?" But they had. Rowaida and I tried to connect, Sigrun tried to connect and that's when we realised that the net had been cut. They had done it. The government had shut down the internet to try and stop the world from seeing the level of police brutality and the rising number of deaths caused by the brutality. The army was soaking up all the attention, pretending to be peace keepers, I didn't trust them. Neither did ramO.

Within the next few hours links were being set up by an invisible team of online activists to enable us all to have internet access. They were sharing the content being sent to them via private offline networks, just so what was happening in Egypt could still be seen by the world. What was happening needed to be seen. Some of the material being sent by text messages was how to reconnect to the net, how to rebuild it, how to overcome exposure to tear gas, both in English and Arabic. Text messages were flooding into my phone from people in England, Egypt and many other countries around the world. People wanted to hear what was going on, and I realised I was the only one they knew in Egypt that could tell them. I was also in connection with many different people in Tahrir. I was getting updates maximum every 30 minutes from various people and so I started to blog about what was going on. I spoke on BBC Radio Sheffield, BBC Radio 5 Live, I was even sent questions from local and regional newspapers back home for more information.

Some of the news that kept filtering through on text messages were about how online activists in different countries from around the world were about to do something BIG. Something akin to the government shutting down the internet, closing the doors to communication and hiding behind their own ugly arrogance. Then it happened. An anonymous source shut down government websites. They were supporting the Egyptian people as the Tunisians had been helped. Even the head of Google, Wael Ghomin, who created the We are all Khaled Saeed, was seen regularly supporting the protests in Tahrir. The people of Egypt were sick and tired of the oppression, fed up of being mindless slaves in an archaic system that valued no one.

As Friday approached, tensions were running REALLY high. After what was now four days in Tahrir protesting and making their demands heard, having had the internet silenced, and Mubarak go on State TV and insult every single one of the protestors with his arrogance and denial of what was happening, even I was getting angry! That Friday became a very dangerous day and went on to be known as the Day of Rage. ramO was so eager to get down to the protests and for the first time since those first moments of planning what to do if anything happened to him, I knew that today was likely to be that day that he either disappeared, got beaten or worse, killed. I had a strange calming sensation come over me though, I knew that if anything awful happened to him, or if he died, then at least he would have died working with others to make Egypt a better place for others, for the generations who had been abused by their president and for the future generations to come. He would be a man of action, a man true to his word, rather than those men that liked to talk and moan and advise without getting their hands dirty, the cowards; like they say, "Live by the sword, die by the sword."

This was the day that the main headquarters of the National Democratic Party was set on fire, and boy how it burned. There was no democracy in Egypt and this building was an insult to democracy, so I am not surprised it was burnt down. The photos ramO showed me later that night when he came back were amazing. I mean love a bonfire, a campfire and fireworks, and no I am not a pyromaniac, but to see the flames in their intensity sent shivers down my spine, because it wasn't just about the fire, it was about what the fire represented. The depth of corruption, lies and mind games, the deep seated manipulation, the oppression and the suffering that the government had subjected the people of Egypt to, going up in flames. The people had hit back, and they had hit back not just in the defiance of their strength to congregate and protest, making sure their voices were heard nationally, but this time globally, but they had defied every warning issued by the government and now they had set fire to the NDP headquarters, the backdrop of Tahrir square where everyone around the world could see. This was a massive up yours to Mubarak and his vile regime. Massive.

Turning on the news was becoming a ritual. I would occupy the boys with activities and then sit down to do 'my work'. After a while I had to stop, and decided that the boys and I needed to get outside. But we couldn't. At the end of the driveway to the apartment buildings was a group of men from the other buildings who had armed themselves with machetes, scaffolding poles, long blades, wooden posts, anything really that they could keep everyone inside safe. Who were they protecting us from? The police. The army were now being put out on the streets in masses. Tanks were rolling by along the corniche and now you'd hear people chanting that "the people and the army were one." People were giving the soldiers flowers, taking photos of their children with the army, but it just didn't feel right to me. I've never been a fan of the army, in any country, and most certainly not here in Egypt. I knew this was another great lie and betrayal directed at the Egyptian people. Adbel Nasser, although he was loved greatly by the people, he betrayed Egypt in many ways when he was in power. He was incredibly charismatic, but he was an enemy to his own people, and to his fellow Arabs, especially those in Yemen.

Whilst watching the news, there was an announcement that we were all being put under curfew, home by 7pm otherwise pay the consequences. Well, how I laughed! I had never in my entire life had a curfew other than "home before dark". Growing up in a village was ace, you knew you were safe because most of the people in the village knew who I was and who my parents, grandparents and aunties and uncles were. There was no need for curfew, and for the government to issue a curfew was, yet again incredibly insulting. Who the hell did they think they were? Curfew indeed! And 7pm? What? Not happening, and I seriously mean not happening! For one, I was still running around the car park at night, with my audience of cheerleaders shouting to me, "Go madame, go madame!" I needed that run, even though it was becoming more and more dangerous, I needed to run off the day's events and clear my head. Very few people took notice of the curfew, and remained in Tahrir. Those that had been camping out in Tahrir since the beginning were arrested, beaten, the camp destroyed and yet, they still returned, more came and replaced the ones that were removed by force.

My love for the Egyptians was growing and growing fast. I was seeing the backbone of steel that had been suppressed. I saw them finally standing up for themselves, for their country, for the future generations. They were growing up. Removing the shackles of the 'daddy' who kept them in line by rule of fear and intimidation. The bully, the abuser and the torturer had to go, and now the Egyptians were doing what was needed to get rid of him. I was so honoured to be in Egypt at this moment in time, honoured to be able to be trusted by the Egyptians that were out protesting, and by those online that were sharing and including me in the news updates of what was going on across the country. With so much anti-foreigner feeling going on, to be anything but Egyptian was dangerous in some parts of Egypt. The propaganda machine was in full force and foreigners were being targeted, especially the journalists. I never considered for a moment that I may be targeted or watched, I was simply a wife sat at home keeping friends and family updated back home in their respective countries, and taking care of keeping my boys up to date with their education. Just because there was an uprising going on didn't mean to say my boys were not going to continue with their schooling. I had enough books and access to the internet, albeit intermittently, that I could make sure they stayed up to date, ready to hit the ground running when they returned to school.

Over the past few days, many residents across Egypt in the various towns and cities, people were looting, food, electronics, clothing, whatever they could get their hands on. Shops destroyed, family businesses destroyed, because it wasn't just the international chains that were in Tahrir, these were family businesses that had been built up over generations, and the sad thing was, this had started to create resentment amongst some of the people. Nor did the fact that the banks were closed and ATMs were fast running out of money, and the bakeries weren't being restocked. The powers that be had already started to cut off the life lines that people needed, but now that State TV had had to acknowledge that 'something' was going on in Tahrir, they reported that it was the protestors that had caused the problems. A way to divide and conquer, just like the Great British Empire. What a great legacy us Brits left behind all those years ago. Those with half a brain cell could very easily work out that it was the government putting a block on everything, how could it be the protestors when they were in Tahrir? What power did they have over the banks and the grain stores? Why would they want to prevent people from getting cash out of the bank and buying bread when they themselves needed money and bread, and were fighting for freedom? It was the ones that were afraid of change, the ones that had been completely brainwashed in thinking that Mubarak was a great leader, the ones who needed the abuse him and his government dished out, because that is all they knew.

A case of Stockholm Syndrome on a national level was really starting to become apparent, and the more I saw of it, the more I began researching it and the wider implications of what it meant if the protests failed. I began reading more and more of the history of Egypt, and the more I read the more I wanted to read. I read about the history of the Arab world, I studied more Arabic, was determined to further my knowledge of Arabic, I had to. It was a driving force within me. No more pretending to speak Arabic, and staying at a beginner level (even though some of the Arabic I knew was very advanced due to integrating into the Arabic world over 15 years), I was going to play full out. I called Sigrun, told her I wanted some Arabic study books, with CDs and a recommendation for learning Arabic. A plan was forming in my head, and nothing was going to stop me from fulfilling it. I wanted to get to the heart of Arabic language and culture, to the heart of the Qur'raan, to the heart of Islaam and I was going to, come hell or high water, I was going to dissect everything I had known up until this point, and build on it. It was game on time.

It was now the 30th January, 5 days since the protests started, and so much had happened. The army had made sure their presence was felt by flying over Tahrir in their F-16s, shaking the ground and trying to dominate. It didn't matter though, the feeling of jubilance was building. People knew things were shifting, and in their favour. The Egyptian people were beginning to realise their power, they knew the world was watching and that the world was supporting them. There were many political games going on, as there always is in any country, but huge progress was being made, and not just in the protests, but in the solidarity of the people. The way people were bringing food and water to the protestors, the way taxi drivers and minibus drivers were giving protestors free lifts to and from the square. Individuals that were driving to and from Tahrir were offering lifts to those walking, it was a beautiful thing. Before 25th January this hadn't happened for years. I remember being in taxi's and others jumping in with you, sharing the ride and the cost, but over the last seven to eight years, this had stopped, and this is when I noticed Egypt starting to decline. Egypt had lost so much of itself over the last five decades. In the beginning of the 1950's when Egypt was a heck of a lot more liberal, and there were more freedoms. Looking at the people in the street you didn't see women in gallebeya[39]'s, unless they were from the lower classes, you saw women in knee length skirts and blouses, bars would be open, and life was more free. Egypt hasn't just been under a dictatorship since Mubarak began his 30 year reign; it has suffered since King Farouk was in power, before he was overthrown by the military in 1952. Through Abdel Nasser's and Sadat's reign. It suffered from international dictatorship during the invasion of the British and the French. The best time for Egyptians went back as far as 1808 when Mohammed Ali, the Pasha for Egypt took over and created the foundations for what is now modern Egypt, the only difference being, he enabled the people, rather than destroyed them. There was over a century of oppression that these protests were fighting, and it brought people out of the shadows, people of all ages, all walks of life, standing shoulder to shoulder with each other. People who had lost their voice decades ago had found them; and they were going to be heard!

Due to this depth of oppression, protestors were now travelling on foot, minibuses, cars, any means of transport to join the protests in Tahrir. The protestors were feeling positive and the mood was a good one according to ramO and many of my friends and contacts across Egypt, which had grown quite substantially over the last few days. Although the BBC were reporting only tens of thousands, there was hundreds of thousands in Tahrir alone, and that didn't include all the other protests happening in the smaller squares around Cairo and the protests in places like Suez and Alexandria. With prisoners now escaping and no police presence anywhere, anarchy really was in full flow.

Egypt Air cancelled all flights in and out of Egypt, now that the embassies had flown many ex-pats home, many like myself hadn't even been contacted, but even if I had, I would not have left. I'd only just arrived and this uprising wasn't going to scare me off. If my family and friends were going to live through it, then so was I. With everything that was happening across the country, the protestors were rallying for a 'Million Man March" a peaceful protest. It was to be on Friday. Friday the 1st, and it was going to be HUGE. It was intended to be a peaceful protest so I wanted to be there with the boys. I wanted to show my solidarity, simply because if I want my human rights recognised, then it is only right that I help others get their human rights

---

39   Gallabeya – the long gown worn by both men and women across the Arab, and the Muslim world.

recognised. Want for others what you want for yourself.

The morning of Friday 1ˢᵗ arrived and I was up and ready to go. Breakfast was made, lunch packed into backpacks, the boys had already been told what was going to happen and they were excited. Flags at the ready, scarf tied in a red white and black sequence to match the Egyptian flag, along with my entire outfit, and off we went as a family to stand for freedom, justice and equality. With so many heading into Tahrir, the excitement was palpable. People were chatting, laughing and chanting we were going on the Million Man March. Finally I got to go and protest, show my solidarity with the people I had grown to love over the last 15 years, for a country that had gotten under my skin. A place I had chosen to be my home. A place I had chosen to raise my children.

We had to get off earlier than normal when heading into Tahrir because the military were stopping people from entering the area. There were blockades made of massive concrete blocks, barbed wire, military checkpoints everywhere. Wherever you looked you saw burnt out cars, piles of rubbish that had been burnt, anti-Mubarak graffiti on walls, the posters of him torn down, it literally looked like a war zone. Naasir being the little action man that he was, kept saying, "Cool!" to everything, he was only four and tanks and guns were more of a game to him, whereas Khaalid was eight and being true to himself was observing with deep interest.

Streets we had walked down only a couple of weeks ago were now destroyed and if we thought there had been a lot of people in Tahrir before, pah! We knew nothing! Getting into Tahrir was a struggle, but an easy one. The boys and I were told by ramO not to speak English near the checkpoints, but once we were through into the main square, people were very welcoming. I had been worried about the anti-foreigner feeling, but needn't have been. I spoke with many protestors, even got interviewed by Sky News and CNN as to why I was there. People were cheering me on and one protestor gave me a big hug after my interview with CNN and told me I was more Egyptian and Muslim than many. I was rather overwhelmed at that point. I mean what do you say to that? ramO introduced me to Jim Muir, the BBC Correspondent for the Middle East. He interviewed me about my thoughts and why I was there. How ramO knew him was a surprise to me, but he knew him. I knew that Jim was based in Beirut, Lebanon, and a year after this interview, I had the pleasure to meet Jim again, this time over dinner in Beirut during Ramadan.

It was a pleasure to meet with him again and spend the next few hours discussing life in general, and how to find a great English-Arabic translator for my up and coming book *Friday Bridge*.

Time passed so quickly during the day and the heat hadn't bothered me as much as I thought it would do, but then again I was distracted by the reason for being there and keeping an eye on the boys. At one point, the boys clocked some children on a tank and wanted to go and do the same, well they wanted to play on the tank full stop! Neither ramO and I were fans of the army, but we asked the soldiers if we could have a photo of the boys on the tank. The soldier was more than willing to let this happen, and slightly confused when we didn't want him or the soldiers in the photo, just the tank.

The boys were getting tired and it was getting close to 5pm, it was time for us to head home. We walked from Tahrir around the back of Garden City, through all the blockades and along the Corniche. There were loads of people walking back with their children, and the camaraderie was great. After walking for about a mile, we were picked up by other protestors heading out towards Ma'adi. The roads were the emptiest I had ever seen them. Normally the traffic is so backed up and congested you can't even see the road, but from Garden City to Ma'adi I counted three cars. I reminded ramO of what the roads were like on the day of Princess Diana's funeral. Once we arrived home, I wrote up my next blog entry and made dinner. The boys chilled out on the couch and ramO got to work on his stuff. It had been a great day, and it was finished off with one of Mubarak's speeches informing the Egyptian people he did not intend to run in the next elections, but would stay and see in the newly elected president 'for easy transition'. He was yet again insulting to the intellect of the Egyptian people and this made them angry. What was he not getting? The Egyptian people didn't want him, even though there were a few thousand that did, mainly those who benefitted from his regime, he had to go, and they were not going to stop protesting until he was gone. He may go on about how he fought for his beloved country. I would really hate to see how he treats things he doesn't love, if this is how he treats a country he does love!

The next day however was ever so slightly different, and became known as the Day of Rage, or the 'Battle of the Camel'. This is when we first saw pro Mubarak supporters arrive on the streets, and they arrived first in Alexandria. Clashes were violent and what had been peaceful protests overall up until now, saw many more injured in this one day, than had been previously wounded in the days leading up to it.

The internet was also now partly restored so using the dial up links wasn't required in most areas, but people didn't trust it. How could TE Data (Telecomms Egypt) have cut the internet? People wanted to switch over to Etisalat, TE Data's biggest rival. But for now, bigger things were at play than switching phone providers.

Around 11am those in Tahrir were warned to leave by the government. They knew of groups that were about to invade the square with firebombs and were going to burn down the square. Of course they knew! They were the ones that had bribed these thugs, and threatened to hurt their families if they did not obey! So around 12pm, Tahrir square was invaded by thugs on camels, brandishing machetes, swords, guns and any other weapon they could get their hands on. Molotov cocktails were being thrown, along with the stones from the pavements and curbs. It was violent. REALLY VIOLENT. It was intense. It was scary. I was sat at home watching, then playing with the boys, reading stories and trying to call friends to see if they knew of anything other than what was being shown.

ramO called to say he'd been hit with tear gas again. He'd been down near Ramsis as well, so had seen quite a lot of bloodshed. He never came home that night, saying it was safer to stay at a friend's house. I was really worried because I hadn't heard from him like I had on previous days. I didn't get to speak with him until about 10pm that night. Hearing his voice was a relief. When he came home the next day, he looked tired. Drained, but fired up. Stronger. The photos he showed me later were crazy. I couldn't believe what I was seeing. I hugged him so tight. So pleased that he was home.

The next day he stayed home and we watched Star Wars with the boys. At one moment during the film, Khaalid turned to me and said, "I think I get it." When we asked him what he 'had got' he said, "Well the Emperor is Mubarak, Omar Sulieman is Darth Vader and the protestors are Jedi." I just stared at him and started smiling, then giggling. He'd just put it perfectly; and at such a young age. Nice one, Khaalid.

The next morning ramO left for Tahrir early. He called me to say he had bumped into John Simpson, the English Foreign Correspondent and World Affairs Editor for the BBC. From that day, ramO was to be working with John as he travelled across Egypt, translating, fixing and arranging things for him. He was also working down at the BBC make shift studios overlooking Tahrir Square, along with many other news teams from around the world. I was proud of him for really stepping up and getting involved. He was fighting for Egypt, whilst remaining neutral in his explanation of things, and he was doing it in his way. He got to do the voiceover translations for some of the news reports John Simpson made, which some of our friends back home in England heard. They said it was one of the maddest things for them out of the whole news coverage, hearing ramO's voice on the BBC connected to such a story. With having had limited access to the internet, and with events unfolding and being filmed live over international TV, people were concerned. Where we okay? How far away were we from what was happening? But they need not have worried, we were doing fine. We were doing what comes naturally, just rolling with the punches. It was good to be working closely together again. Learning to be with each again after so much time apart. ramO had been working on business contracts all over Europe, only getting back every two to three weekends, whilst I ran the businesses and took care of the boys. So, to be together again was taking some adjustment. It was good though, we were getting to know each other all over again.

Once ramO started working with the BBC I was a lot more relaxed. I knew he was in safer hands, and getting to see the much wider implications of the protests in different parts of Egypt. Visiting remote areas and other cities. What were the views of the people there. He was following events as they unfolded. Union workers started joining, arriving in their white Dr coats, lawyers, members of the regime walking away stating they couldn't be part of it any more. Funeral processions were made through Tahrir and then probably one of Mubarak's most insulting speeches to the people of Egypt on the 10th February, where he defied the demands of the Egyptian People, stating he was staying until September. This sparked a fury and you could feel it in the air. It was like a Mexican wave of energy, because even from three miles away, the boys and I could hear the roar of the people. Couple that with the roar from the TV… Oh yes! I felt Egypt roar. It sent goose bumps all over my body. I felt the power shift in the air to one of pure determination. It was time to uplevel again.

This, and demonstrations outside of the media building, demanding honest journalism, resulted in them finally shifting the focus and start supporting the protestors declaring them Youth25. This shift was another sign people were waking up. Those that had sat on the sidelines, or afraid to speak up, were now speaking up. People were snapping out of the coma they had been in, and had found new courage in the fact that they were unified as a country. But the energy in the air, WOW! It still makes my skin tingle thinking about it, that outpouring of determined energy that I felt.

On the 11ᵗʰ February, following more protestors turning up in Tahrir square, and an incredible intense chanting, again which I could hear from our apartment some three miles away. There was fire deep inside these voices. An anger, but positive and deeply united. To be honest with you, whilst writing this, I am having to stop because it is making me rush with adrenalin just recalling it. ramO was out with the BBC again and I spent the day writing and the boys were busy playing with foam swords pretending to be pirates and shooting pretend guns with their fingers. It was a normal day as far as I was concerned inside the Aysha household. Hearing the boys laughter during everything going on was such a joy. That's the amazing gift our children give us. It doesn't matter what is going on in the world, when you hear your children laughing… Best sound in the world.

About 5 o'clock text messages and tweets were coming through that Mubarak was going to resign. These rumours had been going around for a couple of days now, but the difference was, this time it was about who was tweeting and sharing this information. I started to pay closer attention for the next half an hour, then I was glued. I could feel it, this time I believed he was resigning. I started pacing. Getting excited, all those who had died were not going to die for nothing. Their efforts, their voices and their presence had achieved something great. Then I had to calm down, what if it was another insulting speech? AAarrghh… I wanted to slap him! Hard. Across the face. With a shoe. Proper Arab style. But I knew deep down he had resigned. There was a weird shift again in the energy, like an eerie calmness, still high energy though. It enveloped you, like someone wrapping a big positive force field around you. (Yes, I'm a mother of two boys, it's a force field!) Then the announcement came that he had resigned and that the army council would run the country. The cheer that went up was immense! Seriously immense! Three miles down the road, it sounded as though they were all outside in the garden! I remember celebrating with a dance and repeating, "YES! YES! YES!" over and over again! Laughing and dancing with the boys and Naasir asking if the Jedi had won, to which Khaalid responded with, "Of course they have, they are Jedi. Jedi always win. That's the whole point." I giggled to myself again, I loved my boys so much and now that Mubarak had been ousted, it was time to celebrate and get on with making the rest of our future happen. (Nicely played out by the army, don't you think?)

For the next 48 hours parties were had everywhere, fireworks could be seen and heard everywhere. Car horns and whistles could be heard constantly. People were walking about really happy. Big massive grins on their faces, everyone being nice to everyone, it was great! It was also great to be able to leave the apartment for the whole day and get some kind of normality back. Sigrun and Rowaida arranged a get together for all us girls and we were all going to celebrate. Everything was such a blur when we got together. The time line of events and when this had happened and when that had happened. It was only a couple of hours after we had shared everything we knew and how we'd felt about our husbands out protesting, that we were able to really comprehend what had happened, and not just for the country, but also to ourselves and our families. Protecting the kids from the news as much as possible whilst still letting them see what was going on and explaining why people were doing it.

I told them both that I had also decided to send the boys to Narmer (Maadi Narmer School). Sigrun sent her children there and so had Rowaida. Both with different perspectives on the school. That night I made a plan for the next day. I sent emails to Ma'adi Narmer School and requested places for the boys and sent a request to visit the school. I knew it was unlikely to hear back very soon, especially with what was happening, but it was another job done. I still had a book to write and I needed to get things out of the way so I could focus on that. In the meantime the boys and I had fun learning, playing, cooking and cleaning. I also made contact with a woman who I had been given a number for. I wanted to move and apparently, this was the lady to help. So, school and new apartment contact made, now what? Well I wanted to join a local sports club, somewhere we could swim, play sports, chill out in the sunshine in nice surroundings and meet people.

A month later we joined the Ma'adi Sports Club. The boys enjoyed swimming lessons and hanging out by the pool, so did we. I mean come on, being sat by a pool on a hot day with a nice cool drink? Why would you not? We would then take the boys to the play area and work on different things, sharing ideas and giving advice. Both of us planning what we were doing and which direction we were heading. My book was well underway and I was enjoying it. Remembering some really brilliant nights out raving, happy childhood memories, how much I had achieved that I never thought possible.

Also, remembering some sombre moments of my grandparents dying. Converting to Islaam, setting up businesses and working with Channel Four on a documentary. It was mental realising everything I had achieved, the places I'd been, the opportunities that came my way. I was excited and it spurred me on to do more, be more and enjoy more. Seeing all the bloodshed around us, and watching the events continuously unfold was something I became immune to in some ways. I had to be. If I had continued to watch the news and absorb my time with it all, I would not have been able to achieve all the things that needed doing. I also noticed that other people were doing the same thing.

I heard back from Narmer regarding the boys joining the school. They were also keen to know if I was willing to be interviewed for a job as Class Teacher. You see we, as parents, had to submit our CVs as part of the selection process for the boys to be accepted into the school. They saw that I was native English, well read, highly skilled and had studied the TEFL[40] years earlier, and did training sessions for people in business. If I was willing to work at the school, I could start in June and prepare for the September when my boys started. Everything was agreed and that gave me a deadline to really make inroads into my book.

Over the next few months leading up to starting at Narmer, I took some writing jobs at the AUC[41], covering business lectures from senior business leaders on doing business in a post revolution Egypt. I kept thinking to myself, "But it's not a revolution. It's not finished yet." The sad thing is about working for the AUC, they are the worst organisation I have ever done business with when it comes to paying. You'd have thought what with the protests and what people were fighting for would have actually made the people and organisation wise up, get with the programme and sort out their own infrastructure. What made it worse was here I was covering events on doing business in a Post Revolution Egypt and how businesses needed to improve, and you had the very organisation running these events taking 8+ months to pay their freelancers. When you chased them up for your

---

40   TEFL – Teach English as a Foreign Language course

41   AUC – American University of Cairo

money, you were met with all kinds of excuses. Nothing had changed here then, just verbal diarrhea and rhetoric, playing to the masses. The lecturers and students may have been fired up and excited about creating a new way of doing business, but the internal admin weren't. There was no 'whole of organisation' commitment, no synergy. I knew it would take time to adjust but bloomin' eck! Seriously? I remember saying to my friend Eslam a good 18 months later than this, when he asked me to give Egypt time "how much time do you need? You are the second oldest civilisation on the planet and you want more time?? Walaahi?? Idah[42]?!?" This was again another opportunity for insight, many Egyptians believe Egypt was the first civilisation, this is why they call Egypt 'Um Dunnya'. When in fact Sumar was, now modern day Iraq. The lack of knowledge Egyptians have about their own history is shocking. Modern History you can forget about them knowing. Pharonic history is the only history they know, other than how the English and French came over and ruled them.

I enjoyed working for the AUC, and I had started tutoring Mahmoud and a guy called Mostafa for their IELTS exams. Mahmoud was so eager to better himself and help Egypt. His passion and drive for goodness, with a really playful nature was inspiring. He had a sense of romanticism about him, rose tinted glasses even though he knew the depths of evil his government was capable of. For a guy to be so aware of everything, and yet still so positive and enthusiastic, it was hard not to like Mahmoud. He had a really generous heart and such an animated persona, I loved spending time with him and putting the world to rights as we continued to build JCI[43]. We were going to do it, and it was going to happen, because it was a very solid solution for so many of the problems within the country. It's what people were asking for but not knowing its existence. We were going to make sure they knew about it, and we were going to work on getting it affiliated. Egypt would be part of JCI no matter how long it took us. So now I had three projects: my book, JCI and AUC, with being a class teacher of FS1[44] in June. Things were really taking shape.

---

42   Idah – means what, but when used like this it means WTF (What the fuck?)

43   JCI – an international Leadership and Entrepreneurship programme which is built by individual volunteers, who organise and run personal and business development events, on a local, national and international level.

44   FS1 – Foundation Stage 1 – a class for 4-5 year old children

One of the events I covered for the AUC was titled **"How Can Egyptian Firms Manage the Post Revolution Business Environment"**. It was the 3rd debate in a series of MBA debates hosted by Dr Khaled Dahawy, Director of MBA Programmes at The AUC's School of Business.

With high calibre speakers for this debate being Mr Mohamed Mo'men, Chair and co-Founder of the Mo'men Group, Mr Emad El Sewedy, Chief Executive Officer and Managing Director of El Sewedy Electrometer and Beethoven Tayel, Founder and Managing Director of B2LS Consulting, the debate promised to keep Ahmed Tolba, Director of the El Khazindar Business Research and Case Center, as moderator busy. I had no idea who any of these people were and the only name I knew of was Mo'men, a sandwich shop akin to Subway – the 'freshly' made fast food sandwich chain.

These guys were obviously highly regarded as the auditorium was packed event. It started with a "power cut", typically Egyptian and seemingly appropriate given the "power cut" on the recently overthrown President. However, this only added to the relaxed and pleasant atmosphere already in place.

Before the debate started, recognition was given to all of those who had entered a paper into the KCC case writing competition. Of the 33 entries submitted, only 20 were accepted. The three winning entries were all submitted by female students. Dr Khaled Dahawy presented Noha Samara with third prize, second prize went to Wisam Morsi, with the first prize going to Hend Mostafa. Each won recognition amongst their peers, a cash sum and entry into a prestigious business journal, details of which are to be released later on. It was great to see these females acknowledged for their work, but the cynic in me wondered if this was playing into the role of a 'new Egypt'. I was felt a twinge of annoyance in myself for thinking that, but with everything I had seen in the last 8 or 9 months, I was understanding that when it came to Egypt, you should never say never.

The debate itself turned out to be less about how to manage the post revolution business environment and more to do with how each of the speakers had developed their businesses. With the three speakers all taking different roads to great success, it was a very inspiring evening, but what about doing business in a post revolution environment? How were things going to change? What needed to be done? What had we learnt from that had just happened and why people were rising up?

What I did learn though was interesting. Mr El Sewedy informed us he didn't like taking orders from his uncle in the family business and wanted to be in control of his own future, making his own dreams a reality. Describing how his first venture failed and his return to the business market meant he realised "failure is when you decide not to continue" and "success comes from failing due to the amount you learn". A great analogy. I just hoped that those in the audience knew that the fight for a new Egypt wasn't over yet, and that they couldn't get complacent. As Jim Collins says, "People get so complacent being good, they forget to be great." The results thus far had been good, now we needed great. We needed a new government, strong, just and firm believers in human rights. I liked the way in which Mr El Sewedy used his return to education, which made him look at things differently and furthered the understanding of the ideas. He said, "You have to make room for the competition and break the monopoly." Wise words that all future leaders should listen to. Comments such as, "Don't develop something for the Brazilian marketplace when thinking like an Egyptian," and, "You mustn't go global with a local mindset, you have to have a global mindset, whilst remembering to have a global company with a local organization," may hold very important lessons for both new and seasoned business owners, but they also hold true for Egyptians going into a new Egypt. There is no point going into a new Egypt with an old Egyptian mindset. If you want different results, then you need to think differently.

Mr Mo'men described how he grew up in an environment of entrepreneurs, and although his father was against the idea of him going into business, he gained his support in the end. The arrival of McDonalds into Egypt in 1994 changed the focus but certainly not the objective of the business. During a nine year period (2000-2009) of expanding an already successful business by adding a new product line (Three Chefs), acquiring 'Pizza King' and venturing into other countries, Mo'men also underwent many financial challenges with the global economy crashing just one month after an international deal was signed and The Mo'men Group was created. Knowing what I knew about business and how Egypt was divided into many different class structures, I knew that this man here in front of me was an important figure head for business in Egypt. He would have a lot of connections. With the age of his employees, Mo'men would make a great sponsor for JCI Egypt. I had to snap myself back into the room as my mind considered this idea.

As with all things Egyptian, timekeeping was now becoming an issue. Mr Tayal gave us all an account of how after graduating with his B.Sc in Mechanical Engineering from The AUC, he went on to obtain his MBA from the University of California in San Diego. He described his various roles prior to B2LS consulting and how he was adamant that he did not wish to return to Egypt as an employee. B2LS Consulting was born after a plethora of ideas were discussed over email with 24 other AUC Alumi, all of whom wanted to do something positive for Egypt. He was one of the previous brain drains that Egypt saw, knowing that there was no way he would achieve what he wanted to achieve by staying. This was a powerful message for me as a mother of two boys who had planned to stay in Egypt for at least five years, we were already coming up to the end of our first year.

I was still wondering when the topic of "Managing a Post Revolution Business Environment" would become apparent. There was a lot of self-indulgence and not a lot of strategies for the future. It wasn't until the Q&A session that the students, with their hunger for knowledge, started asking questions that brought out some ideas on what the future held.

When one of the students, Ms Noha Samara was told by Mr Tayel, in response to her question regarding starting in business as a consultant "this is not the time to be thinking of starting up in business, especially as a consultant". I couldn't disagree more, and felt it a very negative point of view considering Mr El Sewedy went on to answer the following question "Is it realistic at this time to encourage entrepreneurship or export?" with "It is important to consider all options available. There is a light at the end of the tunnel with lots of opportunities always out there. Egyptians should always look to overseas markets for opportunities as well as here in Egypt." Starting a business now, and laying all the foundations would mean that when things were more stable, this young lady would have already been established and ready to fly, whilst others were just starting out. If these guys were such great entrepreneurs, why did they not understand this basic and simple concept? Karen Millen started during a recession, and if you really want something bad enough, you'll make it work, regardless of what others, and the market, say.

I found the next question quite revealing, especially after the answers given to Ms Noha Samara. When the three men were questioned with "After the revolution did your strategies change?", Mr El Sewedy gave the response, which summed the revolution up perfectly with "It is not enough to stay in your office, you have to participate, you have to put your business and your voice forward". He also went on to stress to students "this is not a time for businesses to downsize. If companies downsize they will not be ready for when the market rises again." So if it is a time for them to be ready for when the market rises, why not those looking at setting up in business? Interesting that he should be discouraging entrepreneurship but preparing himself. Further comments added by Mr Mo'men stressed that "in 2011, sustainability is the name of the game, and so is how to manage your cash. Cash is king". Great advice any time in business, not just in a post revolution period.

In response to a question about whether it's advisable to start new NGOs, Mr Tayel informed us that Egypt has between 27,000 and 30,000 NGOs, but he thinks only 200-300 are active. Therefore it might be a good time to start a new NGO but only if there isn't a successful active one to join. With this new nugget of information, I was determined to contact these three men afterwards to inform them about JCI Egypt and what we were looking at achieving.

A question was then put regarding finance, especially for a start-up. With the then current targets set by lenders and business organisations being as Mr Mo'men put it "unrealistic" for a business to achieve in the short time periods given, it is time to wonder whether business in a post revolution era will diminish the elitist attitude that exists in Egypt's business community at the moment or whether this will be a revolutionary time with people from all walks of life being given the opportunity to succeed. I was keen on seeing the latter happen. Everyone equal to create a business and thrive. My entrepreneurial spirit was on fire. I knew there was a lot of knowledge and experience missing in this room, and I started to create a series of seminars in my head to develop with Mahmoud and the growing team of JCI Egypt.

With the final, and possibly the most important question of the evening, "How do you fund a business and survive corruption?" Hinting at how to overcome the large financial costs of bribes and not becoming part of the corruption problem yourself, Mr Tayel replied "you just get on with it. If you don't know how, then hire someone who does by either giving them a wage, a fee or equity", confirming his statement from earlier on in the discussions "If you cannot find your way out, you are not an entrepreneur". I couldn't agree more and I have to say this event was one that did make me realise just how much my entrepreneurial experiences, and knowledge of doing business in

England was valuable. Top it off with the fact that I also spoke Arabic and knew the culture here, I knew I could benefit businesses both in England and Egypt. Now it was just to figure out what that looked like? What could I offer?

What was clear from the debate was that during this current transitionary phase existing businesses needed to consolidate. The fundamentals of the business environment had not changed since before the revolution, the same problems were still present but with the added problem of the environment being extra fearful, so money supply is more limited (that is not an entrepreneurial mindset at all, and I remember shaking my head at that. Like I said a few moments ago, if you want something bad enough, you'll make it happen. However, the speakers emphasised that the Egyptian economy had not collapsed post revolution, and that when the economy does start growing again it's likely to boom with many opportunities and hopefully much less corruption. Here I sit some six years later seeing Egypt still in a mess... Something the military seems to be willing to continue.

The next few months I had spent a lot of time with Mahmoud both tutoring him and working on launching JCI, delivering events such as "Know what you want and how to get it" and "Managing your time for Mastering your life". I was also delivering training on other subjects such as planning, goal setting, leadership and how to network effectively. We approached AISEC, Al Maqqar and iceCairo all of which were positive. We held events and attracted enough people to build a team. Projects and an events list was drawn up, and I devised a Growth Strategy for the next five years. The problem was we were not licensed, and the amount of obstacles we had to overcome were incredibly frustrating. License fees, scarcity mentality and fear of a new international NGO being set up so soon after the protests; even though there was paperwork going back to months before the protests began. Mahmoud was dealing with the licensing and registration and we were both working on the social media awareness and networking. I was still working on my book and home schooling the boys, so in the months following the resignation of Mubarak I was kept quite busy.

Mahmoud had made contact with a chap called Robert Kesten through JCI, and he was coming to Egypt to develop a Human Rights Corp. We were both excited to meet with him and on Monday 13th June the initial meeting for the Human Rights Corps in Egypt took place. Some were apprehensive about it because of fears relating to extreme characters turning up, others were worried about the meeting being led by an American and others were put off because the event page on Facebook was written in English. All apprehensions and fears were acknowledged and understood, but English was the language of science, maths and business, and the universal language of JCI so the delivery had to be in English. As for the fear of the meeting being led by an American, they needn't have worried. This was no ordinary American. This was Robert Kesten, and his track record in human rights was more than admirable. It has been a long time since I met a guy who has blown my mind within the first meeting. Robert's actions for global Human Rights include working within the former USSR, Korea and many more. For the rest of his achievements and endless work to bring Human Rights to the world, you'll just have to google him. Be prepared to be impressed. I know I was, and not just by his professional career either.

The first of the key points that came out of the meeting were regarding the obligations of Egyptians to the freedom seekers around the world; Egyptians have given them hope, and renewed lost hope, for their own freedom. The second key point was that democracy is messy, it isn't easy and commitment is needed. A fear that came from one of the Egyptians present at the meeting was "although the methods used by PDHRE are great and will work, they will only work for the middle classes. Human Rights also come about through the labour market and through social justice. The people in Tahrir were not only shouting for democracy, they were shouting for 'bread, freedom and social justice'. Many people will still be swayed by the political parties if they are given bread and clothing to feed their starving, and in some cases homeless, families, even if they do not agree with the politics." In fact, PDHRE's work is designed to reach all people regardless of class and once Robert had discussed this point, and explained what had worked in other countries, fears were being dissolved.

One of the aims of the Human Rights Corps of Egypt was to have organisations commit to implementing Human Rights into their organisations. Once they have made this commitment, they would be able to send individuals from their team to the Learning Process meetings in Cairo and Alexandria. Alexandria was really running with the idea, but those in Cairo were not so enthusiastic. The Learning Process provides knowledge and deep understanding that Human Rights is a way of being, not just the newest

fad for business. One of the key points that had to be made was that human
rights had to be taken seriously. One of my concerns was organisations such
as Amnesty International were not allowed an office in Egypt, so how were
we going to make this work? Especially when we learnt each meeting ideally
needed 40 individuals to be in attendance, each representing an organisation
that services a whole community, literally 1000s of people. This way Human
Rights could gather momentum, and with the work being done at the grass
roots by other organisations within the labour market, the goal for Human
Rights to be an intrinsic part of life, "just like speaking", would soon be a
dream realised and Egypt will become a powerful and successful country
with respect, justice and freedom for all the people living there at its core.
The thought of this was exciting, and would solve many of the problems
we had all just been involved in the protests to highlight. I contacted many
friends and contacts I had made since arriving, but soon realised that one
of the biggest problems facing Egyptians right now, and something that
will hinder the growth of any Human Rights actions, is the suspicions of
non-Egyptians wanting to help. One individual noted prior to the event that
it is "a bit weird" that someone who is not Egyptian would want to help.
For me it is "a bit weird" that anyone who believes in Human Rights and
democracy, would find it "a bit weird" that someone not indigenous to a
country, wouldn't be interested in the Human Rights of the country. If you
believe in Human Rights, you believe in it for everyone, not just yourself and
your fellow countryman.

Another problem that was identified as something that would hinder the
development of Human Rights in Egypt is the consumerism of the middle
classes. Many of the middle classes do not "wish to trouble themselves",
many just turn a blind eye to the problems and others just are not interested
in anything but looking good and feeding their own egos. Many are feeling
unsettled because they are no longer judged on the clothes they wear, the
clubs they attend, the cars they drive. They are being judged on their part
in the revolution and their political views. Whose side were they on? The
revolution had given the world a new view of Egyptians and many who have
never been interested in politics, were now finding themselves caught up in
something that has them feeling way out of their depth.

Whilst speaking with one of the guests at the event, I was informed that
those who wished to make a difference, those that wanted to help people

out of poverty, were on the ground working with a variety of initiatives. Egyptians, and Arabs from across the MENA and Gulf regions, were reclaiming their identity. Many of them increased the amount of Arabic they were using on social networking sites, and some had gone as far as apologising for using English. Egyptians were now delivering speeches in Arabic for the first time in a long time. So progress was being made, but the sad thing for me, was I couldn't join them. The fear and rejection of endeavours by foreigners had elements of xenophobia, but like I said before, I understood the fear and rejection. I dislike a lot about British colonialism, but I am not them. I may be seen as a middle class British woman, but I am prepared to go to jail if it means standing up for Human Rights, anywhere in the world, not just in Egypt. I just wish many of the Egyptians knew that 'we're not all bad' and accepted our intentions as good ones, and not there to 'patronise and take over'. Some of us genuinely want to do our bit for the sake of our own children, grandchildren and great grandchildren. The world is getting smaller every day, and with the US and UK having been at the top for so long, we have to remember that there is a circle of life and the only way to go from the top is down. It's better for us all to work together, learn from each other and drive Human Rights forward in *all* countries, not just for ourselves to enjoy.

Egypt needed to keep moving forward, because settling for stability was not the answer, resting on their laurels wasn't going to be the way forward, and failing in democracy would only lead Egypt to a failed revolution such as the one in Russia. Russia doesn't have a real democracy, its economy is based on the sales of oil and arms, and it's unstable.

I also needed to keep moving forward, and I was due to start at Narmer school in Ma'adi. I was looking forward to it. I had always toyed with the idea of becoming a teacher, but as I had never been to university to study, I didn't have a teaching degree which had stopped me from becoming a teacher in the UK. Now though, thanks to the number of native English speaking teachers that had left during the early days of the protests, I was able to fulfil a long forgotten dream. I was going to be a teacher! Of the little one! I was so excited!

My legacy to Egypt

During August we moved into Ma'adi Degla, one of the nicest ex-pat areas, It was opposite signa Tora[45] and looked over the ground of the prison, and the link road from the Cornice to the ring road to New Cairo. It was a great apartment, and a great location. It didn't have a bath, which was a massive negative for me, but the rest of the apartment was positives all round. I could live with just a shower. The prison grounds were not as bad as they may sound. There was a grave yard behind the prison wall, which we could see because we were on the seventh floor. There was also an ostrich farm within the prison wall and I regularly saw prison officer riding horses around the prison grounds. Many Egyptians hated the idea of living near graves, but like I said to them, they were quietest neighbours I'd ever had! No trouble whatsoever.

The great thing about living where we were, was we were a 15 minute walk from the Nile, 10 minute taxi ride to school and back, and a 20 minute walk to the club. Shops were less than five minutes away, and there was an Arabic language centre just around the corner, not to mention another book shop less than five minutes' walk away. I was pleased with the progress we had made. We'd had achieved the three major things I had wanted to for us as a family, now it was about leaving my legacy in Egypt as me, as Dawn Bates, not as a mother, or a wife, but as me. What could I contribute? By being the best FS1 teacher this school had ever had, and shortly after we had settled into the apartment, I was getting ready to start at Narmer.

---

45   Signa tora – Tora prison – where Mubarak as supposed to being held

Arriving at the school the first day I was ever so nervous. I was actually an employee for the first time in nearly 15 years, and that came with mixed feelings. I was also going to be working with children, and you know what they say… never work with children or animals! But I loved kids. Loved being a big kid, and I had great things planned.

On the first day I was introduced to a young woman called Amira. I loved her from the moment we met. She had such a wonderful energy and I knew we were going to make a great team. Our kids were going to have a blast in class, as well as learning a huge amount of knowledge. I also met a woman called Rehab, who was going to be the art and music teacher, and Summay'ya who was the Arabic teacher. We all got on really well. Throughout the first week, we were given our objectives for the year and told to create lesson plans for each term, as well as around each topic, and theme. We were also given booklets with activities and worksheets within, and given an order form for class decorations. Amira and I chose the Super Star theme, and some monkey stickers. She didn't know what the monkey stickers were for, but she would do.

Amira and I chose to go out for coffee together on the way home from school to discuss our ideas. I knew part of my role was to train her up to be a teacher, so I told her that she would be leading a lesson every week. She was so happy about this, as well as nervous, but I knew she would nail it. She had that energy about her. We sat in Cilantro along the Nile near Ma'adi Mall and drank iced coffees after iced coffee's and were laughing so much the guy behind the counter kept looking over at us. I heard Celine Dion come on the music player and had a cringe moment and whilst laughing I asked him to change the music. When he asked why, and we got into a discussion about love songs such as the ones from Mariah Carey, we all ended up laughing. When we went back the next day, our drinks were already waiting for us. Bonus! Great customer service. I liked it!

By the end of the second week, we had to submit our lesson plans, I was slightly nervous, again. Never before had I been so nervous. What was wrong with me? Other than it really mattered to me. For me there was a lot riding on me being the first teacher these children had ever had. How I performed and taught them would shape the way they remembered school, not just now but in the future. I wanted them to love school, to love learning and I hope that had come across in my plans.

My Head of Department Iman Badawi had been really friendly and supportive of me. As she went through my plans I could see her face change, and we could feel her energy turn to a negative one. When I asked if the plans were okay, I was met with a "Yes. They are okay, they are more than okay. They are very good in fact" I was as pleased as punch! First time planning a whole year of lessons, five per day, across all subjects and themes and we had done a fab job! So why wasn't she happy? Rehab, the art and music teacher, felt the negativity too and just smiled at me. Maybe I had misread the vibe, but I didn't think so.

Amira and I went about organising different things in the classroom, our theme walls, the layout of the classroom once the furniture had arrived. We were having a great time. We obtained the materials we could to make our own resources and we continued with her training. After about 6 weeks we were ready to go. I had created spreadsheets ready to record letters sent out and reply slips returned, books borrowed and a whole host of other records that would help me keep track on each of the children. I printed off all the plans that we were going to be working on daily, weekly and monthly and pinned them up on the board by my desk so Amira and I had a 'quick glance' system to keep us on track.

When it finally came to meet the students I was unsure of how to greet the parents, let alone the children! What were the formalities? Did I shake the hands of the dads? When the mums reached into greet me with a double kiss on the cheek greeting, was that acceptable... I just chose to go with the flow. Whatever happened, happened and if I got in trouble for it, then so be it. The Arabic teacher Sum'maya that was assigned to our class, take the lead during the first hour and had us all holding hands and skipping around the classroom. I watched her and I learnt very quickly. I was still greeting parents and some of the later arrivals, joining back in with the skipping around the classroom. I was giggling with the kids and I just knew this was going to be a lot of fun.

There were two children in the class that didn't speak with anyone much, they were the shyest ones, Salma and Mohamed. I remember it taking me nearly 5 weeks to get a response out of Salma, but when she responded to me in English I cried with joy! She'd done it!! I was so excited!! Mohamed was chatting the next day and he became my cuddly bear. Every morning he would be one of the first to arrive at school. At first he was sleeping, but as term progressed, and the year progressed I learnt that he was being a cheeky little monkey and pretending to sleep so he still got to cuddle with me in the morning. That was okay though. I always arrived at school with my boys at 7:15am, so not only could I prepare the classroom and have a quiet cup of coffee before school started, but also so my boys could enjoy the playground swings and slides, not to mention the whole playground. Working at Narmer was a blessing for us all in so many ways, especially with the outside space. I could see why it was a favourite with parents who could afford it, and were willing to travel as far as they did.

Each morning my little helpers, in the form of Ali and Karma, would bring not just giggles to my face but also tears of laughter. Ali was one of the most outspoken, cheeky little monkeys I had ever come across. He was adorable and proper little businessman; always negotiating his way around things, attempting to talk you into letting him do something or talking you into doing something. I fell in love with this little boy hook, line and sinker. As for Karma, well she was the second teaching assistant in the room. Whenever a task was coming to an end and I would stand at the front of the class to get attention, Karma would spring out of her chair and request "FS1, look to Ms Dawn". She would look so proud of herself, and it always made the class giggle, and take notice, so I allowed it to continue. Each of my pupils had a little job to do, hence the monkey sticky labels I had purchased. I asked Amira to explain to our class matron Heba, to print the names of all of the children onto the labels and then laminate them. I also needed green ribbon to make the neck ties. Heba did a great job with everything we needed. She was such a lovely young woman and very conscientious. She had such a talent that I told Amira that if Heba wanted to learn English, I would be happy for her to sit in all our lessons and learn with us; and if she needed anything from me, she could have it. Amira translated this and Heba smiled such a beautiful smile. We used our monkey badges for school trips as well as our leader badges, so that whenever we went somewhere my class were able to be identified. We had so much fun in our classroom. Everything from combining science, maths and English to make cookies and cakes, especially when we were looking at changeable and unchangeable states, more or less, squares and rectangles as well as the colour brown. I'd hit upon a great idea of making chocolate brownies, and boy did they go down a treat. The kids really remembered that lesson!

We hung artwork on the walls, creating 3D effects on our farmyard wall, a park and play area for our maths wall made entirely of different shapes which the children had to identify, and remember as the board began to build a story as the weeks and months passed. We hung butterflies, dragonflies and papier-mâché bugs such as ladybirds from the ceiling using fishing wire and hooks. Asking the school bewaab for fishing line and hooks and asking him to put them up for me did confuse him, but by the end of the next day he saw what Amira and I had created with the children, and he loved it! All the support staff loved my classroom. It always smelt of baking, on a Thursday and it was always the cleanest classroom. I had taught my class that there was "a place for everything and everything in its place". Each wall in our classroom had on going evolving theme boards, and each time the kids left the classroom for either PE, Art or Music, Amira and I would get to work hanging up or displaying more of the kids work. After school I would grab the paints and add to the theme walls something new for the next day, or completely update the theme boards ready for the new topics. Seeing their faces light up in the mornings when they came in was such a beautiful sight. I was becoming addicted to these children!

I also taught them that if they made a mess, they would clean it up. It was what grown up boys and girls did, and they even came up with a song that they sung at the end of each messy lesson. "Clean up, clean up, everybody clean up". Even if the class wasn't messy, all the crayons and books were put away nicely, and books collected in by one of the little leaders chosen for that day. Amal the head matron, loved coming into our classroom and seeing the children cleaning up their mess so all she had to do was go over it with the disinfectants. It made her job much easier, especially as she had to do all the classrooms in a very short window of time. I loved Amal, she was such a wonderful lady, and couldn't do enough for FS1, Amira and I.

My little leaders wore their monkey badges on the day that they helped me and Amira with chores in the classroom, and they would wait each day eagerly to find out if it was their day to lead. Ali always helped out, regardless of whether it was his day or not. He didn't have a very long attention span so I would break his tasks down into smaller sections, and he would be so eager to come and show me his work. Many told me that he was a handful, and yes he was in many ways, but he was also an adorable young man.

Due to the different interests and skill levels I had the children teaching each other. For example, my 'mini me' in class Farida (proper bad ass this one! A fighter and a young lady who is going to go very far in life. Nothing and no one is going to stop her… she is Farida! And boy did you know it!) She loved colouring, she loved climbing, she loved sports and many times when she ran, she fell over because she was leaning so far forward and her legs were going so fast she couldn't keep up with herself. She also was a strong powerhouse who stood up to the boys, which they didn't like, but which I supported 100%. She was a leader, and she knew it. I had her be my art leader, teaching Zein, another cheeky monkey how to extend his choice of colours. I would have Ahmed and Zeina working together on Maths and English as Ahmed was a whizz with Maths and Zeina was first class at English. All my students were becoming capable at reading the letters and by the end of term one, they were able to tell me how I had punctuated a simple sentence on the board incorrectly. Writing the sentence incorrectly on the board and getting the kids to mark it was hilarious. They loved marking my sentences, telling me I had got it wrong, and how to correct it. They loved it even more when I marked their handwriting books and put stickers in their books. Working with the kids was such a beautiful experience. Teaching them to read, hearing them read with ease, and express themselves was magical. I realised I had helped give these beautiful children the gift of reading, a gift that would enable them for the rest of their lives. One young lady, and she was indeed a young lady, and also one of the quietest, Layla Mohamed, was a fine reader. She was also my most eager student. She wouldn't just complete her homework and her reading that I gave her, but she would also complete pages in extra books that her mum had bought her.

I remember all the children in my class, especially a young lad called Bilal. I think his transformation was one of the biggest. He was a quiet little mouse when he came to my class, and by the time I left the school, he had found his roar of a lion! He was a very talented artist and loved drawing so much. Mostafa was another one who stole a piece of my heart and I loved how he would get so excited, jump up and down with a proper Wallace[46] smile on his face – he was such a joyful and appreciative young man. Absolutely adorable.

Lots of the other teachers were really friendly towards me, but the better the results I was creating the more I felt a distance from a few of them, especially the ones who had been teaching a long time. When I was in the

---

46   Wallace grin – Wallace from Wallace and Gromit. And a smile from ear to ear, pure joy.

staff room, after I had done all my marking and Amira and I had gone over our plans, I would pull out a text book to study. It would either be a book on learning breakthroughs, how boys and girls learn differently or how to improve classroom management. I was loving this learning process, especially reading the Michael Gurian books.

Outside school, things were great. Khaalid and Naasir were doing really well in their swimming lessons, football sessions and we spent a lot of time inside the club. I started running around the track and found it quite amusing that some people were just using it for a walk in their shib-shibs[47] whilst on their phones. Why do that on the running track? Idah? Walaahi?

I was enjoying the running, and kept pushing myself harder and further all the time. I also joined an adults swim team. Nothing serious, just a little fun. We competed against other sports clubs and I was chosen to swim backstroke, which I am pretty good at... when there is a ceiling, or bunting above the pool. Put me on my back in a pool with no markers and you have a wandering swimmer! I was all over the place! Swimming into the left lane partition, straightening up, only to go into the right lane partition. Needless to say it was good fun, and I didn't come last like I expected to. I had probably swam twice the distance than I needed to with all my tangent swimming, but hey, who cares!

The build up to the elections was in full swing and all throughout October, November and December all people were speaking about was whether Abdul Fotouh was going to beat El-Baradai, Mohamed Morsi or one of the other candidates running for President. El-Baradei was a considered not suitable to run for Presidency due to the large amounts of time he spent outside of Egypt, but he still played a large part in the narrative that was ongoing, and would continue to be so. He had to be, he played a large part in the ousting of Mubarak with his political comments, he had previously had ties with the Muslim Brotherhood and he was a Nobel Peace Prize winner, author and he had links throughout the world. He was globally minded and lots of people like him, but did they like him enough? That was the question.

When the election results came in stating that Mohamed Morsi had won and Ahmed Shafik had lost, I was relieved. I had dreaded someone like Shafik winning because it would be as if nothing had changed, the protests pointless and all those lives lost for nothing. Recounts were ordered, voting

---

47   Shibshibs – flip flops

slips were found on the roads down to Suez, and cries of rigged elections. It was becoming a bit of a farce to be honest. During the elections, we had so many days off school. The school administration were worried about the children getting to and from school. I didn't understand it, and told Amira that I didn't understand it. How come the kids in Palestine and other parts of the world still go to school, but the Egyptian kids were told not to go… just in case? I had been over heard by someone and it hadn't landed well. I also couldn't understand the nastiness directed at some of the more conservative members of staff. The important thing was: were the kids learning? And whether they liked their teacher. I had many different views on what was going on across the country and the world, and when asked about my views, I would decline to take part. I had already sensed a distance from other teachers, and I knew my political views wouldn't do me any favours. Best to keep them to myself.

It didn't really matter though. I would go into the staff room and all of a sudden they would all stop talking, or they would switch from English to Arabic. I would go in other days and they would just completely blank me. I just said 'toz[48]!' and went about my day. I would get some really lovely messages in the daily planners from the parents, including one that appeared in Farida's planner "Farida was being naughty last night and so I told her that if she didn't behave she was not attending school tomorrow". I giggled at that one and looked directly at Farida who was watching me like a hawk, trying to figure out if I was going to have words with her. I let her stew for a bit and when I walked past her, I asked her if she liked coming to school. When she looked up at me and smiled, my heart melted. I loved this little girl so much, and I was one of the only people to understand her. Farida was a tom boy, and in Egypt, girls were expected to be girlie. The only really girlie girls I had in my class was Malak and Dalia. Yes, Leila Tamer was girlie, but she was also a tough cookie. She was incredibly anxious when she first started at school, and there were moments in the first three months that if I left the classroom this little girl would cry her eyes out and scream. She had very good reason to as well. What I learnt about this little girl shocked me. Something I struggled with for a long time. I sent her mum info on how to deal with the death of a parent, but it fell on deaf ears, and I was pulled into

---

48   Toz – whatever! Fuck it! Who cares… there isn't really a hard and fast explanation of this word as it works in many contexts.

Iman Mattar's office, the headmistress, for interfering in Leila's life. When I informed them her anxiety was impacting the rest of the class, it became my business, and the business of the school. We had to support her through this transition, not ignore it. So one of the strategies I put in place was marking the workbooks during either Summay'ya or Rehab's classes. I wasn't welcome in the staffroom at this point, so marking the books in my class was the right solution for Leila and for me. After a short while though, Summay'ya made a complaint about me and I was escorted to Iman Mattar's office again. She was beginning to see a pattern that was occurring but what could she do? She had to investigate all the complaints. It was becoming a daily thing being complained about, and some of them were so pathetic, I had trouble believing grown women were capable of such childish antics.

A few of the reasons I was being ostracised was because my FS1 class was outperforming children in Year One; and Iman Badawi, my Head of Dept, was teaching FS2, the class above mine. Naasir was in her class, and so I knew what he was learning. I informed her he was completing the homework really quickly and asked her for more extension work, but it never appeared. In some areas such as spelling and handwriting, my class was also outperforming Year Two. This didn't help matters. Then it came down to the training we were doing. Amira and I were a team. She marked books, led lessons, and we developed all our presentations together. We presented together and every Monday after work we would head to Crave, a really nice local restaurant for vanilla and espresso milkshakes and a bite to eat. We worked our way through the TKT[49] course and kept our KPIs up to date. I was also really organised. If ever I was asked for something, there was a spreadsheet for it. Iman Badawi started to try and catch me out, but I had become aware of her little games and refused to play them. More and more, I was being called into the offices of both the school Principal Reham El Kammah, and Iman Matta's. It was getting ridiculous, especially as I was being called out of lesson to deal with the pettiness. The kids started to notice something was wrong and that upset me more. Some of the things I was accused of, you just couldn't make it up.

One day I had had enough and just broke down in tears. Rehab and Amira comforted me and told me that I was not to worry. They also told me that Iman Badawi had had it in for me since the day I had submitted my

---

49   TKT – Teachers Knowledge Test (Cambridge University)

plans for the year. It also didn't help that I was British and they assumed I had been put on an English salary, which of course wasn't the case. I had told Reham, the Principal that I would not be happy taking a salary higher than the other experienced teachers simply because I was English. That didn't sit right with me. The other teachers also didn't like the fact that I was British and could leave any time I liked. The victimisation had got to such a point that the children had noticed how the other teachers were treating me, and speaking about me to the children in their own lessons. Summay'ya, the Arabic teacher, would say things such as, "Ms Dawn doesn't love Egypt. She's not Egyptian. She can leave any time she wants."

Seif, one of my students had been really upset by this and asked me why I didn't love Egypt. When I told him I loved Egypt very much, which is why I chose to live there, even though I was born somewhere else, his little face lit up. I was upset that the adults in this environment were, themselves, behaving in a more childish fashion that the children themselves. There were a lot of bitchy comments about the fact that when I went home most nights, there was a delicious meal cooked for me and the boys by ramO. He worked from home so he made dinner some nights. They only found out by chance when they asked me what I would be eating for dinner that night and I said mou'sa3'a[50] They said I wouldn't be eating until late, and it was my reply of, "Oh it will be ready for when I get home, ramO is cooking." To me a perfectly innocent reply, but to them… something completely different. Not only have I got a British passport and could leave anytime I wanted to, and I was married to an Egyptian (who chose a British woman over an Egyptian) but he also cooked for me?! That just wasn't on! That was enough to create a rapidly growing green-eyed monster in most of them.

They also tried to tell me how to behave in accordance with the Qur'raan, but having studied it, I was able to ask them to prove where in the Qur'raan the instruction they were giving me was. None of them could. They didn't like the fact that I had done my research. I knew as much, if not more than them, and they hated it.

Outside the school things were hotting up with the Presidential elections. I was being interviewed by the BBC back home in Sheffield and JCI was moving in the right direction. My book was coming near to an end and I was

---

50   Mou'sa3'a – mousaka – a traditional dish made with aubergine and ground beef. Absolutely delicisou!

also swimming a lot. I was also spending a lot of time with Gitanjeli and we had organised a Ramadan event of cooking 500 meals for the homeless and handing them out. Gitanjeli was the main driving force behind the cooking project, and at each halaqa that we attended, other sisters had bought supplies or more donations of cash.

I had been continuing to go to the halaqa but I was realising I just wasn't interested in the religion as much as I once had been and was taking on a more freeing acceptance of belief, of soul, of spirit. So many religions had so much beauty, and although I still believed in a higher entity, I wasn't as bothered about the framework religion gave. I had been debating whether to take the scarf off or not, and how I was feeling about my faith. There was so much going on that I was reflecting on what I wanted in my life, who I wanted to be, what I believed in. I was doing a lot of soul searching, making sense of everything I was reading, experiencing and seeing. Developing my knowledge of Arabic was also helping me.

It wasn't just that I wanted to stop wearing the scarf, it was about how I wanted to live my life, and I didn't feel the way I wanted to live my life was in line with Islaam anymore. I had deep, deep faith in our Creator, and still had a close affinity to Islaam, but I just didn't want to be defined as a Muslim anymore. This was something I kept close to my chest. I got out of praying with the girls by 'being on a period', and I missed so many prayers due to the amount of work I was doing. I felt I was constantly playing catch up, and for me that is not what having faith was about. Surely it is my belief in a single Creator that is important, and my daily actions being positive ones that counted. It had nothing to do with whether I prayed, or drank alcohol, or smoked weed, it was all about what positive impact I was having on the world, now, and in the future. Looking around me I saw loads of Muslims, but again the more I delved deeper into what faith meant to me, the more I was being pulled away from organised religion and deeper into a private spirituality. The questions Haylie Winter had asked me during the making of the documentary series 'Make me a Muslim' with Channel Four, had been resonating with me strongly. I couldn't shake them off. Faith was a private thing, not something you declared to everyone.

Back in school, Iman started to set me up to fail, by giving me more classes, setting tighter deadlines, expecting me to deliver more in shorter time frames. I had already taken on doing the morning line up and exercises whereby we would sing the national anthem, and do a 10 minute workout. I had also taken on the drama classes, and requested at the last minute to lead the Arabic, music and art classes. I had not been provided with any lesson plans, so I just went with the flow. I kept delivering and the more I delivered the more it pissed her off, but I wasn't going to not deliver and have her use it against me. In the Arabic classes, the children loved that I spoke Arabic, because when it was my normal lessons, I wasn't allowed to speak Arabic, so for them to hear me speak Arabic resulted in them giggling away, because to them it was strange and naughty. We had been told on numerous occasions not to speak Arabic in my normal lessons, so for them to be in class, with me, speaking Arabic… it was amusing to say the very least. In the art lessons I had the children drawing and colouring different instruments and labelling them, and in music I had them choose their favourite songs and play the instruments in their favourite songs. We also learnt songs and made up our own.

The refusal to let me mark homework and workbooks in certain places, had gotten to the point where I was told I could not mark the kids work in the classroom, so I had to find somewhere else. So I marked the work out in the playground on the benches near the gardens. It was blissful, I was outside, nice cool breeze and meeting lots of other children from other classes and the national division. I got on really well with all the children and they found it amusing because some days I would have leaves in my scarf, along with twigs and flowers. They were gifts from my class at break times and I would wear them like a crown. This made the kids incredibly happy, but alienated me further. I was told I wasn't allowed to mark work outside any longer, so I went to the library to mark the work, then I was told I wasn't allowed to mark the work in the library, so I stayed behind after school and marked them. Although it was an upsetting time outside of the lessons, inside them was magical. Watching the kids learn and grow, read book after book and start eating healthy meals was so enriching! I had implemented a daily food challenge "Fit not fat" to help them understand food groups, healthy eating and of course reading and spelling. I would say to them that small changes make a big difference. I wrote home to tell the parents what would be happening in line with the 100 days of school theme Narmer ran. I would be giving the children a star each day if they had carbs, protein, vitamins and minerals, as well as a healthy drink, and the one who got to 100 stars first would get a prize. This was received very warmly by the parents and many of the messages in the planner were ones of thanks, not just for what I was doing for the kids, but what I was also doing for their waist lines! Soon enough the kids would be excited to tell me what was in their lunch boxes and could name lots of different foods in each food group. If a child had received a star each day of the week, we were in school, then they went up on the 'healthy heart, healthy me' board, where they had a passport sized photo stuck onto a heart shaped piece of red construction paper. I was going to inspire them to take care of their bodies as well as their minds.

Another of the great joys, and another reason so many parents loved me, was because I would host birthday parties in class, and implement the learning objectives of the week into the party. So for example we would develop listening skills by playing musical statues, we would learn colour patterns by colouring in birthday cupcakes on an activity sheet. We would also play a whole host of boys v girls games built around words, numbers and colours of the week, or we would get them to play dress up, such as on animal day for Bilal's birthday. Zein had a Peter Pan party, and Farida had a PE party. Each party was designed around learning and accelerated the results that kids generated, and we had great fun! One of the games was a cross between hang man and cup cake decorating. I had chosen a lot of three and four letter words each with a letter missing. The kids had to decorate the cakes with the missing letter and then put the cake in a certain place on the desk. Once all the cupcakes were in the correct place, they would spell out Happy Birthday! And the name of the child. Bilal's family didn't celebrate birthdays so we had Bilal Day instead; he loved it! We all did. School was wonderful inside FS1, but outside of the classroom, it was awful. I hated it.

I was asked what I thought on many occasions on various subjects, but due to the increased spitefulness of the other teachers I declined to get involved in the conversation, other than with one or two. Sarah Magdy, a teaching assistant was one of the five people in the British Division in Narmer that I got along with, other than Amira. Naneece was the other teaching assistant. Both really lovely people and very supportive. They had seen how I was being treated and offered solutions and advise. The other three were Ahmed, Karim, and Rania. Ahmed was a dude, a complete dude. He played the guitar like a proper bad ass and invited me to the Cairo Jazz Club to hear him play. This is when I met the lovely Osama and Yehyia. I loved the jazz club and went there a few times. It was to become a regular place for me towards the end of my stay in Egypt. I was changing. My view of the world was changing. How could it not with everything I had experienced thus far?

Karim was the PE teacher and invited me to take part in the lessons, which I gladly did. The kids loved that too. There wasn't much I couldn't do to make my kids laugh and run and hug me. Rania was a fellow English teacher and although we had a shaky start, we are still dear friends to this day. There were others at the start of term that I had really connected with, like Soraya, who was there for a short time only. She was shocked by what she saw happening in the school, and the way both I and Amira were being treated, and because she chose to be friends with me, they turned on her too. So she left. She wasn't going to be part of the negativity. When she left, she gave me her class terrapin. He was called Monster. He was kept in class until half-term holidays and then I took him home. He remained with us in our apartment until he died. It was horrible seeing him dead in his tank, especially as he had been with us for nearly a year when he died. One of the things I saw which was so blatantly on show, was the weakness of the people who follow the crowd, the moment one person takes a dislike to someone, the weaker ones follow, especially if that person is in some sort of power position. I had never seen this in adults before, and if I had, never to this extent. Sarah and Naneece wanted me to train them as well but it just never happened, in part because diaries just didn't match up, but also because I was resisting teaching them as I didn't want any more hassle. I was given a warning one day by one of the teachers in the national school to watch my back as Iman Badawi was very good friends with Reham, and Iman didn't like the fact that my class, although a year younger than hers, was out performing hers in leaps and bounds. I already knew this though, because Naasir was in her class. Naasir was always wanting to do more homework and who was I to stop someone learning at a pace they wanted to learn at? So I headed down to Sigrun's bookshop and brought a load of books. I had also worked out a deal where all my students would get 10% discount at The Bookspot, just because they were my students. I would recommend certain books to the parents, that would enhance the learning we were doing in class with the kids. The parents loved the little discount membership cards I made for them to use. Sigrun liked it too. She had a lot more business.

Iman had it in for me, and she was doing everything she could to get rid of me. She had been managing me out since the beginning, but I was still there, and I would remain. I was there for the children, not to be liked by the other teachers. If I made friends, then great, but I wasn't going to half my performance just because someone else couldn't be bothered to step up, or work together as a team so we all became stronger. There was no team work, and this was highlighted one morning when I arrived at the school to be greeted by a flood. Arriving at 7:15 as I normally did, I walked around to my classroom, classroom 101[51] would you believe!? and saw all the downstairs area flooded. This area was like an open-air corridor and was in an L-shape in front of all the classroom doors. If the flood had gotten any worse, then it would have gone into the classrooms and caused damage to work and the furniture. So, I pulled off my Ugg boots, rolled up my jeans and grabbed a mop from the matron's cupboard (which to be honest with you angered me. The matrons for all the classrooms had been given a broom cupboard to rest in. There must have been at least 10 of them, led by the wonderful Amal, and in this cupboard under the stairs were their cleaning products, a little kettle and a place to eat and drink. The way these ladies were spoken to and treated by the teachers and admin staff was disgraceful). Back to the flood before I digress… I had been sweeping away the water with Amal and another matron as teachers were arriving, and instead of helping us, they just stood there staring at us. Then Iman Mattar, came over to me to tell me off for helping. When I asked why she was unhappy with me, so told me it was not allowed and that I may get sick. I didn't get it. I told her that we were nearly done but she told me I had to stop straight away otherwise I would get another warning. Soon some of the school bawaab's and other matrons came and took over from me, allowing me to go and get dried off ready to lead the morning anthem and exercises. There were a few of the other teachers that thanked me because I had taught them a valuable lesson, there was even one teacher who posted a long status over Facebook about what I had done and the lessons taught that we were all equal and how we should do more to help one another. Still confused. Why had helping to clean up a flood that could have damaged classrooms and our kids work be such a big deal? Amira told me she was proud of me for helping, but needed to explain to me why it was a big deal. No one in the school had ever seen a teacher help the matrons, so the fact that I regularly cleaned the classroom with the

51   Room 101 – a term for the bin as exampled on the TV show Room 101 where celebrities are asked to put certain things from society into the bin aka Room 101

kids before they came in, and gave first refusal on the cookies and cakes etc that we made in class as a thank you to them for helping us every day, and then to help clean up a flood was a big no no. It just wasn't the 'done thing'.

I was beginning to really see the bigger picture, about bloody time really! Although the protests had happened, and people were fighting for justice, freedom of speech, democracy, better living conditions, many only wanted it for themselves. The fact that these teachers, and the original JCI board had dismissed the beladi as the wrong members, I was realising that status in society of an individual meant the class they were born into, would be the class they would remain in. There was no chance of progression, not because they didn't have the desire, but because those above them, did everything to keep them there, and anyone who helped them or treated them as an equal was a trouble maker. Forget that these people were Muslim, which meant they should believe everyone was equal, the reality was the same as written in the book *Animal Farm* "We are all born equal, but some are more equal than others".

What with Iman Badawi singling out Naasir and excluding him in from answering questions or helping in other ways, there was only one more nail left to put in the coffin for me at the school, and it came in the way of Khaalid starting to be singled out by his English teacher Ms Ghada. She had told him at the beginning of term that if she got anything wrong, he was to help her get it right. Khaalid being Khaalid and used to me honouring what I've said, and them both being allowed to call me on things, the day finally came when he did as she had asked him to do. It was a simple thing such as pronouncing a word, and when he corrected her, she hadn't liked it. There was also a boy in his class that had taken a dislike to him as Khaalid had over taken him in class, and as he was the son of one of the senior officers in the army, he had taken it upon himself to throw his weight around. When I approached Ghada for an appointment to see her with ramO, as parents, rather than a colleague, she didn't like it, I wanted the boys out of the school because if the teachers were singling out my boys, just because I was outperforming them, then what else would they be prepared to do? I was seeing a very sinister side of the Egyptian people, and it wasn't good. Everyone had their place in society and those further down the 'food chain' and I was obviously being pushed out of place in this school, so much so that I spent most of the time away from everyone marking and studying. Heba, my specified class matron was fired for no reason, Amira was being targeted with questions and comments, pulled into meetings to be questioned about me. It was horrible to see them targeted like this, but again, I was not going to back down. I was not going to stop delivering my best, and I was not going to kiss their backsides. I had a duty of care to both my students and to my boys, so ramO dealt with the boys schooling.

Shortly after the Spring term started, Amira and I were introduced to a new teaching assistant called Leyla Khalid. She seemed lovely enough, but I didn't trust her. Why was she here? Why had they employed her for my classroom. What with events happening outside of Egypt, and all the goings on in the school, I was beginning to get paranoid. Had Leyla been hired to spy on us in the classroom and report back to Reham? It took me a while to trust Leyla, but I couldn't help it, she was adorable, and took her work very seriously. One day though she was very angry, well by Leyla's anyway. I asked her what was wrong and if there was anything I could do, and she just blurted out, "Ms Dawn, I don't like the way they treat you. It is not fair. You are a wonderful person and they just can't do this." She was clearly upset by what she had witnessed and had even spoken with her mother about it. She was determined to help me in anyway, so she would stay late after school and help me. Having both Amira and Leyla supporting me was a blessing.

ramO dealing with the issues with Naasir and Khaalid in lessons had made his own threats to the school about how they were treating the boys, and how it had better stop; it did, but I was fired. Well, I was released on full pay at the end of term two.

A meeting was called for the parents to come into school to be told the 'truth' about me. Now bearing in mind, I had become very good friends with two of the parents and all the other parents really liked me, because their children loved me, and the results in happiness, confidence and abilities their children had gained in the last two terms at school. During this meeting the parents were told things about me that were so far from the truth the parents didn't believe anything that was said to them. One parent was so disgusted by what she was being told, not just by Iman Badawi, Iman Mataar and Reham El Kaamah, but also by a teacher that had befriended me at the beginning named Shahira, that she recorded the meeting on her phone. To hear what was being said about me made me cry. How could they do this? How spiteful and insecure were these women? Then I had a flashback to something an

Egyptian friend in England had told me about Egyptian women "we are one of the most spiteful group of females on the planet. Many of them will love you, but many of them will hate you. Stay strong, stay true to who you are and rise above it." So I did. I went to collect my wages every month from the school, and each time I went I managed to sneak in a little gift for my kids – a packet of marshmallows. It was our thing as a class. A week of healthy lunches and they were allowed marshmallows. They would know they were from me. What I didn't know was that the kids had been told that I no longer wanted to teach them and that I had gone back to England. I hadn't realised this until one of my friends in the national division handed over the marshmallows to Amira the first time and one of my little boys said, "It's Ms Dawn! She's back!"

I was invited to several of the birthday parties of my kids after I left and seeing the kids for the first time after I was fired on full pay was very emotional. I hadn't known whether to go or not, but Dr Rana, young Mostafa's mummy had pleaded with me to go. So had Yasmine and Sarah, so I went along. Some of the parents were shocked to see me, and they too had thought I had gone home to England. It was a mess, the kids were upset, some traumatised so much they started bed wetting, another screaming if left alone even for a couple of minutes, and all because of a group of spiteful women and their egos and insecurities.

The silver lining to this though was Soraya, had highly recommended me to her mum who worked for Collins Educational Publishing. They wanted me to write some educational IT books with them. All the plans were drawn up, all the characters approved and learning levels agreed upon, but then the project stopped. No reason given, and no payment either. All that work, and that time and nothing to show for it. I was gutted, but I was determined to continually develop them on my own time. I enrolled Amira into the idea and she was on board, but life took over and it became a project for the future.

Whilst this Collins Project had been evolving I had been in talks with another school, and as the Collins project came to an end, being Year 3 English teacher and form Tutor at EBIS[52] in T'Gamma Khaimis, New Cairo was confirmed. It was a school I had been looking at for the boys, had heard good things about, so being offered a job there was an added bonus. I was hesitant due to what had happened in Narmer, but surely it couldn't get any worse?

---

52   EBIS – Egyptian British International School, part of EAIS, the Egyptian American International school, owned by Ms Bassouni.

There was still a lot of military on the streets, but the adoration for them that many had had, was dwindling again. So many had seen through their political games. With the run up to the election campaigns, the energy was positive. Dialogue was productive rather than destructive, and so much excitement about what these elections meant for Egypt. They were the first ever diplomatic elections to happen in 5000 years, so whoever won this would have an added layer of prestige. In June 2012, Mohamed Morsi was signed in as President, and what a great thing that turned out to be. Roads were being fixed, street lighting repaired and things had really started to relax. Friends who worked for utility companies were telling me they were so busy being instructed to fix and replace generators and water mains that hadn't been taken care of in decades. No wonder there were so many power cuts all the time, everything really was broken in Egypt.

I have to say though, the boys and I loved it when there was a power cut. They would excitedly grab the candles and have a debate about who was lighting the candles. We would then sit around telling stories to one another and one day I started a Mildred story, that even today the boys ask me to tell them the next instalment of what Mildred is up to. (Mildred is a fictional character by the way in a mildly scary story with lots of episodes made up from three words from each of my boys, and woven into a story). Sometimes we would get marshmallows out and toast the marshmallows over the candles. We loved marshmallows!!

After leaving Narmer, I started to build my tutoring clients and over the course of the week, I was tutoring two nights at home for four: Mahmoud, Mostafa, Ahmed and Mohamed. Ahmed and Mohamed worked for Sigrun, it was a great group to tutor. I also worked at a language centre two nights a week, and a Saturday. I was teaching English to mixed classes of male and females, and of different ages at the language centre around the corner called U-Can. They got me work teaching English in some of the larger independent oil companies. It was great. I got paid in Arabic lessons for me and the boys and what was left owing to me was paid in cash. I really enjoyed this work, and looked forward to walking to the centre for each session. My students loved my lessons and were hungry to learn more. All of them always booked into the next level with me.

I started tutoring Zein, Farida and Ahmed from my class after hours. Zein and Farida were at my home every weekend, and not just for lessons. Zein's mummy Sarah, and Farida's mummy Yasmine spent a lot of time with me drinking coffee. We would hang out after the Friday tutoring sessions, head over to Beano's a coffee house akin to Costa on Road 9. We would go out for dinner at Fudruckers burger bar with the boys. We hung out at the club. We even chose a spa in Zamalek to go to for the day, and boy were we in for a surprise! The female masseuse was a big burly woman and we were given a bundle and told to go into the steam room. Yasmine and I went in together and Sarah went into her own steam room. Yasmine and I kept our t-shirts on and put on the spa knickers and when the masseuse came in, she took one look at us, shook her head and said "Yalla!" She then pulled at our tops and told us to get them off, muttered something to Yasmine and walked out. I don't know who was more shocked Yasmine or me! We looked at each and both cracked up laughing. Here we were two grown women, scared in case this lady came back and told us off again. We felt like naughty little school girls, but I tell you what… that massage was probably one of the best massages I've ever had! (Other than a massage my friend Hale gives, proper hardcore Iranian massage!) These Eastern women know how to massage every tight knot from your body and leave you so relaxed you never thought it was possible.

I also stepped up more with JCI and we were putting on more and more events, gaining traction and Mahmoud was travelling all over the place globally meeting with other JCI members from around the world. We met Fuad Kastali from Syria, Fred Dubee who was an ambassador for JCI USA and shared with them our ideas for JCI Egypt. They did everything they could to help us develop JCI, and with the new team in place, strategies in place, Mahmoud headed off to the International Annual Conference to gain potential affiliation. When he came back with it we were buzzing. One more piece in the jigsaw puzzle completed.

Back to life.

Life was pretty easy going these days, and we were settled. ramO had his projects that were taking him away for TEDx talks, Start-Up weekends and attending seminars which he was writing reviews and articles about for an online technology magazine for entrepreneurs.

During the time off school with their endless days off, which in my opinion were totally unnecessary, the boys and I would travel to Fagnoon with Sarah and Zein, Yasmine, Farida and her old brother Hamdy, who I also tutored privately. The Friday tutoring was fab, and one of the highlights of the week. The boys got to play with Hamdy whilst I tutored Farida, and sometimes Zein. And then it was Hamdy's turn to be tutored. Hamdy was in Year Three and I had the impression he was not getting the support he needed. In the sessions with me, he performed really well, at home he had X-Box syndrome where he just wanted a break from school homework and the extra work with me. I totally got it, but getting the right grades was essential in Egypt. There were so many people going for very few jobs so those with the highest grades, the right background, the right parents got the job, regardless. When Yasmine arrived, we would always spend at least another hour drinking coffee and she would update me on my kids from FS1.

Every third Saturday of the month was spent down at The Bookspot for Bookclub. Rowaida normally read a new story that had arrived that month, created activities around the story and depending on the age category of the story, Khaalid would either join in or grab a book of his own. He, or shall I say we, had really enjoyed a series of books called The Ranger's Apprentice. We had started it when we first arrived in Egypt and we were waiting for the next one to arrive; along with a load of other books. Getting books into Egypt proved hard as so many of them were checked for content. It was crazy. In science books in Narmer, the reproductive organs had had stickers placed over them so the children couldn't see them. In my mind that just made the kids more inquisitive. Many hours were spent in The Bookspot, it was a cool place to be. Costa Coffee was right next door to the left, and Baskin Robbins was next door to the right. The boys and I also loved a café called Mugshot. They did the best lentil soup and pizza, and it was a really nice quiet café with loads of space. The team were really great too.

As July arrived, it was time for me to start work at EBIS. As a staff member, I would get collected from within Ma'adi, by sharaa' Silky[53]. On the first morning, I was stood at the bus stop and noticed another woman standing there. We got talking and we realised we were about to start at the same school. Her name was Noha, and she was English Egyptian, and lived in London prior to living in Egypt. She was very keen on photography and would be teaching English to Year Two, whereas I would be teaching Year Three. We went through really intensive training and it helped us to get to know the other teaching staff. We were a real mix of teachers from all over. Some of our training was combined with the American section of the school, but mostly the British section. My Head of Department was called Reham, and the Key Stage leader was call Mai. The class teacher of Naasir was called Debbie and she was from Scotland. She had lived in Egypt for a number of years and had worked at EBIS for about 5 years. One of the longest serving non-Egyptian teachers. There were lots of us newbies and it was great to be learning together. The school didn't have a garden as nice and natural as Narmer, but it was spacious and had newer equipment.

We were taken to the library and shown where the books were that are students could borrow. I asked when the books would be arriving, seeing so few books on the shelves. The librarian looked at me and asked me what books. I replied with "the books, for the children to borrow". She informed me that the books I saw were the books for the students. I was shocked. I had more books at home, and I was only providing knowledge and fiction for a family of two adults and two children. How could a school library cater for two different schools, one British and one American and have so few books?

---

53   Sha'raa silky – wire/cable road – silky is used commonly to mean electric cable, which made sense as there were lots of gas and electric companies around this area.

My question got back to Reham and I was called into her office. She asked me why I had been rude to the librarian, when I told her I hadn't been, she informed me that several members of staff had heard me be rude. Walaahi! Was this happening again?

A week before the students were due to arrive, we were given our class lists and I noticed that my two classes were predominantly boys. My mind sprang straightaway to the books written by Michael Gurian (The Minds/Purpose/ Wonder of Boys). I knew I had to develop the way in which I had planned to deliver my lessons. Upon meeting my classes, I was delighted with them, especially my form class. There were two boys in particular that I took a shine to, Omar and Hamza, both for very different reasons.

One of the things I noticed about these kids was the levels of obesity in them, not badly, but noticeably so. Seeing their lunches, and the stuff they bought from the tuck shop each day, frightened me. These kids were unhealthy, apart from one or two, and to be honest, no wonder so many of them were diagnosed with having ADHD. I didn't get that they were ADHD, especially considering the crap they were eating and the lack of activity they were doing each day. I decided that my classes would be active learning and I would use the outside space as much as possible. Many of these kids travelled for two hours on a bus, sat in class for eight hours with only one forty-five minute break, before travelling back home again on the bus for two hours. Then many of them were taken to the club whereby they would have to do some kind of training, eat dinner and do their homework. Some of these kids were so full of sugar due to the sweets and cans of coke/pepsi they drank, that they were just buzzing the whole time. They were also very tired.

It didn't take me long to figure out, that these kids in Year Three were really far behind the national curriculum, even for ESL[54] students. They didn't know how to decode words, they didn't know certain spelling rules, nor did they have a Year Three level of vocabulary.

As part of the homework requirements, we were required as teachers to set weekend homework. I decided to create some reading packs, spelling packs and various vocabulary packs. The kids were excited to receive these and were looking forward to doing them as they contained word searches, hang man, word dials, simple grid words and short paragraphs which had 'match the word to it's meaning' quizzes. These activities were targeted at Year

---

54   ESL- English as Second Language

One and Two students. My Year Three students found them challenging. I decided to find out why.

What came to light was really sad. These kids had gone through four teachers last year and during the last term that had had supply teachers for each lesson. There was no consistency at all in the teaching staff and the damage was done to the kids. I also found out that this class had also had three teachers and lots of supply teachers during Year One. They had had no consistency at all. They were playing catch up, and I needed to get them back on track.

My first assessments and reports had caused massive problems for the parents as they had all been led to believe their children were A grade students. They weren't, nowhere near it. At most they were a C, most were a D and the parents were not happy. I was able to back up my grades with the Cambridge Syllabus that we were using in school and show the parents why their children were not A grade students. Many accepted this reasoning and my promise to get their children up to standard effectively and quickly.

The next day I was called into Dalia, the Principals office. I was in such trouble. Her face was like thunder. How dare I tell the parents that their children were not A grade students? They paid a lot of money for their children to be A grade students. I had learnt to hold my tongue in the last place, but here I was told that the school here was very different and we were to be open and honest, so I was open and honest. I told Dalia that the parents weren't paying for the kids to be A grade students, they were paying for great teaching and for the children to be the best they could be. That, as you can imagine didn't go down too well. I was given my first warning. I couldn't believe it. I was shocked. Walking into the staff room Noha clocked me, and her face asked if everything was okay. I told her I would tell her later. Next thing I knew she was in Dalia's office. And so it continued.

Debbie, Naasir's teacher told me she was so impressed with Naasir, it was great to have a child as smart as him in the class, and he was cheeky with it. Yep! He sure was! Khaalid's teacher was equally impressed with him, but was concerned about him as his level was so much higher than the other kids in the class. She wanted to know how far she could extend his work. I told her to extend it as far as she thought he could handle. She was happy to do so. Both boys made friends very quickly and we were enjoying the school, other than the few mishaps I had already had with regards to the library and the grades. I made friends with another teacher Lisa, who worked in the American section of the school. She was Canadian and was having a difficult time in the American section of the school. Listening to what she was saying was like listening to the problems I had faced in Narmer.

Noha and I had experienced a few visits to Dalia's office for a variety of reasons, nothing major. Although the funniest one had to have been the halawa sandwich incident. I had been doing my best to teach my new kids the same 'healthy heart, healthy me' and 'Fit not Fat' content.

One boy had gone home and told his mum he no longer wanted halawa sandwiches. His mother had come to school the next morning demanding a meeting with me, Dalia, Mai and Reham. When I found out what it was about, I found it hard to keep a straight face. They were all insisting that halawa sandwiches were healthy and there was nothing wrong with them, and how dare I attack the Egyptian Cuisine. Walaahi? We were going to spend this much time and effort on this complaint?

Now, for those of you who do not know what halawa is, it is sugar, sesame paste and sometimes pistachios. Some brands of helawa added all kinds of other stuff in it, but this is basically the crux of it. The slices of halawa in the sandwiches were at least a centimetre thick. I had no problem with the kids eating what they wanted, but I wanted to give them the information to make informed choices. This young lad had made an informed choice and here I was in Dalia's office, with three other members of staff and an offended mother. Such a different reaction to the parents in Narmer.

The next day Noha was called into Dalia's office and it was almost as if we were playing a game of office tag. Trivial, pathetic reasons until one day one of the children in my class complained to her dad that I was being mean to her. He was an army officer and it was as if I had just committed a crime the way in which I was frogmarched to Mai's office by Reham. When I got there I was virtually interrogated without being given the chance to answer. When we had got to the bottom of what had happened, it turned out this little girl didn't like doing her grammar lessons and didn't like getting homework. She would often get behind in class due to constantly messing about with her stationary, and trying to distract others in class around her, bragging about what she had done, or been bought at the weekend, and as per the class rules that everyone else followed, any work not completed in class would be completed in addition to the homework set at home. I was given a warning for bullying this child. When I went back into the classroom, this girl looked up at me and knew that she had caused me problems. She started crying. I didn't know how to deal with her tears especially after what had just happened. I told her not to worry about anything, to go to the bathroom and dry her tears. Everything was going to be okay.

The next day I could hear shouting from Khaalid's classroom which was across the corridor from mine, and I mean shouting. We all looked up surprised to hear it and I told my class to just get on with what they were doing, it wasn't our circus, and they were not our monkeys. This put a smile on their faces and I put some music on in class to drown out the noise of the shouting.

Later that day when I caught up with the class teacher in the staff room to ask if everything was okay, she was beside herself. Not only were the kids in her class incessantly rude with her, one of them, again an army officers child had started throwing his weight around in class and was insulting her and other kids in the class. Khaalid gave me more info later that night and said he wasn't enjoying the class because of this lad and a few others who just wanted to mess about. "I just want to get on with it mummy". The next day Noha was really stressed out. Her teaching assistant hadn't come in again, and a few of the children in her class needed additional supervision. One of the boys had bought a knife into school, not very sharp, more of a butter knife really, but he'd been waving it around in class. When Noha had attempted to take it off him he stood up to her and told her, "You can't do anything about it. My dad's in the army." Noha was very much like me, not impressed by people's status in the world. You were either a nice person or you weren't, simple as that really. You could have all the prestige and money in the world, but if you were a bitch or an asshole, you were still a bitch and an asshole, and not welcome in our lives. She managed to get the knife off the child, took the child to Mai and left her to deal with it. She got into trouble for leaving her class unattended, even though there was a matron standing in for her whilst she escorted this boy to Mai's office. A few days later shouting was heard coming from Khaalid's classroom again, so music went on and my class continued to work.

At break I saw Khaalid outside the classroom doing his work. I was surprised at this and asked him what was going on. He told me he would tell me later at home, but he didn't need to. I was hauled into Dalia's office again and there sat Mai and Reham. I wondered what I had done this time and the first words spoken were, "Your son attacked a girl in class today." Total disbelief. I mean TOTAL disbelief. Khaalid didn't like violence, was very protective over girls, anyone younger than him (except Naasir of course, they had their fair share of wrestling and brotherly fights) and babies. Khaalid was not one for attacking anyone. So I asked what happened.

What transpired was during a group working session, each child in the group had been assigned a task to do, they had all agreed on a subject together and moments before Khaalid and this other young lad was about to present the groups work, which was going to go towards their end of term grades, this girl had told them she wasn't going to allow them to present what they had done because she wanted to do something else. Khaalid had told her that she couldn't have everything her own way and that she was selfish. Him and this other lad got up to present and she had stood in their way. Khaalid asked her to move, she didn't so he pushed her out of the way. This account was told to me by more than half of Khaalid's class, but what had then happened was the class teacher had given into this girl and Khaalid had protested that him and the other kids were going to be losing marks in their final assessment. The male warden for the British division had gotten involved, called Mai and here were three grown adults, half the class and the young screaming and shouting at Khaalid. Khaalid had pushed his way out of the class to get away from it all, and had been given a week's worth of isolation outside the classroom. The other children in the class were split in two now, the ones that supported Khaalid and the ones who supported this girl. It turned out that this girl, whose father was a general in the army was known to be a trouble maker and yet none of the teachers did anything about it, because the last teacher that had tried to isolate this girl was instantly fired. Being part of a group of people socially that included lots of teachers from different parts of Cairo, came in very useful at this point. I remember sharing what had happened thus far in school with one of my friends Emily, who worked as a teacher at Amgad Islaamic school. She was not surprised in the slightest with what I had said. She said it was very common in schools, especially since the uprising that military kids got away with everything. You see the thing is, school owners were afraid of the military either getting the school closed down or knocked down; and schools made a lot of money in Egypt. A lot of money.

If you took all the income that this school was receiving, and then looked at the salaries, deducted overheads etc, the school was left with an obscene amount of money that would enable them to equip the school with the many things on the ever-growing list of supplies the parents had to pay, including the toilet roll for their child to use in the bathrooms. All the stationary had to be provided by the students themselves and teachers had to buy their own classroom decorations and provide their own resources. I hadn't even been at this school a month and I knew the boys and I weren't going to stay.

During the run-up to the first lot of exams, I went onto the Cambridge website and researched how to do exams for maximum understanding of materials learnt. I created the exam based on providing the kids stuff I knew they knew to give them confidence as well as stuff that they knew, but would need to think about a bit more. I wanted to make sure the rules and other elements of syllabus we had learnt, they understood by being able to apply it to other texts. I handed in the exam to be assessed by Reham. Later that day she came into my class and told me to redo it because all the material was new material. When I explained the words may be new but the level is correct, the rules and syllabus were the same, it was just transferring the knowledge to make sure they had understood it. I had to re-write the exam because it was not material they had seen before. The school were only interested in the kids relying on memory and not actually understanding what they were learning to be able to transfer the knowledge. The exam day came and we had to invigilate the exams in other classrooms. I was given a Year Five class to oversee, and I had done this kind of work before as a Police Assessor back in the UK. I set the expectations of behaviour, the time and then the kids began the exam. They kept stopping to ask me how to do things, and I was surprised. So I wrote on the board, "This is an exam to test your knowledge. NO help will be given."

At this point a girl burst into tears, then another and who should show up outside the class I was in? Mai and Dalia. They came into the classroom, rubbed off what I had written on the board, Dalia took me to her office and Mai stayed to help the kids in the exam. I was told under no uncertain terms, was I to upset the children during their exams. It was a stressful time for them and we needed to support them. Naasir and Khaalid's teachers commented on how neither of them were stressed about the exams, I asked them, "Why should they be?" For me it's just a marker of where they are at and the areas we as teachers need to help them with, ready in time for their next assessment or exam. It's as much about our teaching as it is about the kid's performance, plus so long as they did their best, no one could ask anything else of them. As the last exam was about to happen, I went to the classroom I was invigilating in, taken into account my warning earlier on in the day, I explained the rules and wished them the very best of luck. As the exam came up to ending I warned the class they had five minutes left, at which point one girl (the one who had gotten me into trouble previously because of my 'bullying') burst into tears. When the exam time was up, I told the class to put their pens down and stop what they were doing. Many carried on. I asked them again to put their pens down and all but this one girl did as they were asked.

Now through the exam I had seen her messing about with her stationary again, looking out of the window and colouring in pictures. It was her exam time, her choice what she did with it. When the male corridor supervisor walked passed he saw her crying, came in and asked me why she was crying. I informed him she wanted to continue with the exam as she had not finished it. So he sent one of the matrons to fetch Mai, who came along to the classroom, and you've guessed it, I was frog-marched along to Dalia's office again, just because I wouldn't allow this girl to go over the exam time allotted.

By this time, everyone in the school was used to seeing me frog-marched to Dalia's office. It was becoming rather amusing to be honest. What on earth could it be this time. I mean I wouldn't mind being disciplined for something I had done wrong, but seriously? Walaahi? Teaching kids to be healthy, to make informed decisions, assessing them accurately, teaching them responsibility? How were these things wrong? When I got to Dalia's office I was really not bothered whether she fired me or not, so I said, "You know what, I should really get a desk here in your office."

To which she replied, "I'm sorry?"

I came back with, "Well I seem to spend as much time in your office as you do, maybe we should just share an office?" This didn't go down to well and I was yet again given a warning for upsetting this young girl. Just because of who her dad was. If your father wasn't in the army, then expect your child to be punished for stupid little things. So many of the kids in my class kept their distance from this girl because of the problems she was causing me.

Parents at the Parents evening were praising me so highly with the fact that their child had gone from hating English to it being their favourite subject.

They had all gone up at least two grades and the parents were so thankful to me. The praise was given by some parents in full ear shot of Dalia and Mai who had been hovering close by.

One mother, who had come from Syria told me in front of them that if it hadn't have been for me coming to teach in EBIS this year, she would have left the school. Schooling in Syria was much better, deeper and richer in the learning, and she was thrilled for me to be teaching her child. Another told me that since I had taught her son what was healthy and not healthy and given him the information he needed to make informed choices, he had become more active and had stopped taking medication for ADHD (which I knew this boy did not have. He just needed more exercise, less processed food and something to challenge him). The high praise and positive feedback was really getting to Mai and Dalia and the parents could tell, but again they were behind me because of the difference I had made to their child.

As it was exam time, it was customary to bring in a dish of food to share amongst the fellow teachers in the classroom. Now I love wara' 3einab[55] and baba ghanoush[56] so I made those and took them into the staffroom. The older Arabic teachers were really impressed with whoever made them, when I said thank you they were shocked and asked if I had gotten them from a shop, or had someone else made them. When I said no, I made them, they were really impressed. There were loads left over, not just of my foods, but of everyones, so I asked if anyone was interested in taking any. Everyone said no, so I scooped up all the food and took it to the matrons.

I had never seen this matrons room, but I was about to have my eyes opened again as to how matrons were treated. There were around 12 matrons, all crammed into a broom cupboard in the toilets. I had seen them here but just assumed that they were getting things from this cupboard to clean the toilets. Never did I think that this is actually where they had to congregate, each their foods and rest between each lesson. I gave them the food and noticed that they were drinking out of jam jars. When I asked one of the teachers why the matrons were drinking out of jam jars, I was told because they are matrons. Only teachers drink out of mugs and cups on school property. I felt physically sick. What the hell kind of attitude was that to have? I was disgusted. And these teachers and admin staff call themselves

---

55   Wara '3einab – vines leaves stuffed with rice, meat, tomatoes, garlic, herbs and spices

56   Baba ghanoush – smoked and mashed aubergine with tahini (sesame paste)

Muslims? I could sneeze out more Islaam than these people had got in their entire bodies. They may be able to recite the Qur'raan but they didn't understand it at all.

The final straw came after I was hauled out of my office by the male supervisor and told Mai wanted me again. One boy in my class shouted out, "Why can't they leave Ms Dawn alone? We love Ms Dawn!" This boy was told to be quiet and given a detention.

What transpired was following a conversation with one of the girls in my class who struggled in class to do the work, but her homework was exceptional. She was also always really tired in class so I had asked her what was going on. She told me that she was training for a big national gymnastics competition and was training really hard. I told her she should have told me, and we could have sorted something out together. When I asked her who did her homework, she dropped her head. I asked her if her mum did it and she nodded. Now the thing is, the way in which EBIS had us grade the homework was based on Accuracy, Presentation and Time, so provided the work done was accurate, clean, tidy and well-presented and handed in on time, it didn't matter about the effort, or who did it. I had sent a note home asking the mother not to do the homework as it was not fair on this child and it was also cheating.

Next day, where was I frog-marched? Yep! To Dalia's office, with Mai hot on my heels. I was given the riot act, and I just couldn't help but sit there and wonder how the hell these people slept at night. As teachers we have a duty to educate these kids and enable their growth, and here they were doing the exact opposite. The fact that Mai wore a headscarf and was a 'proud Muslim' was laughable.

Once the drama of exams were out of the way, it came down to doing the end of term assessments, so I had been making sure my kids had been aware of how they were being marked. Any of them that were behind on work, must get it handed in. I had also put a tray on my desk of work that had no name on it, and asked them to check which was theirs and name it, so it could be graded and handed in. Going through the grade sheets I was really pleased with the results my kids had achieved. All of them had vastly improved in their reading skills, especially reading out loud to the class. They were eager to learn, and we had a lot of fun. Many times during class I would find Dalia, Mai or Reham staring through the big window into my classroom watching my classroom management. I also found other teachers looking through the window.

When I asked one teacher why her and others were looking she simply smiled and said, "Because what you have done with those children is remarkable. They have been a really disruptive year group and you were given some of the naughtiest children in the school, but look at what you have done with them. It is a beautiful thing to see Ms Dawn". At that point she gave me a hug and I cried. I actually cried. Then I got angry. It was Narmer all over again. Do a bloody great job and watch those above try and crush you, well I wasn't going to be crushed. That teacher lit a fuse within me that day and I knew I wasn't going to leave these kids without an explanation to their parents.

I wrote a letter to them all, highlighting the fatal errors of the school system in EBIS and why I was leaving. Noha knew I was leaving, so was she, but at a later date. She agreed to hand out the letters to my kids on my last day. Whenever that was going to be, but it would be soon. Sooner that I had expected. That night whilst walking out of school, Mai called me into her office again and let rip. Man was she a ferocious animal! Reham sat next to her smiling so smugly that she oozed an ugly arrogance.

Mai was having a go at me due to the fact I had written to the parent of the young gymnast asking her not to do the homework. She also told me that what was going on wasn't cheating. "How the hell is that not cheating? Of course it is cheating! The mother is doing the work for her so she can get the highest grades."

Then Mai explained to me what cheating was and all I could come back with was, "When I start telling you what the words in your native language mean, then you can start telling me what my native language means. You're all cheats in this administration. You steal education from the kids, you steal money from the parents in over-inflated fees and deliver nothing that resembles a good education, and you call yourselves Muslims? You are a disgrace to Islaam! No wonder Egypt has so many problems if schools as 'prestigious' as this are as poorly run as this one! You should all be ashamed of yourselves."

The boys were already waiting for me outside, and Noha was shocked by what had happened, and by what I had said, but I was done. When the boys and I got home that night, I told them the next day was our last day in the school. We had discussed homeschooling as an option over mealtimes many times in the last few weeks, and plans had been put in place for when it was time to leave. I was waiting until the end of term, but after this, I really had had enough. They both looked really happy. Khaalid was bored, annoyed he couldn't just get on with his learning and Naasir was bored because the work was far too easy. They were excited about being homeschooled, and I was looking forward to teaching them.

Due to the fact my class had had so many teachers, and they had caught up and were doing really well, I felt awful leaving but I knew this school was not for us either. I had to do what was right for my boys and my own sanity. I had been working really long hours, falling asleep at the dinner table, marking work, creating resources, all for the sake of other people's children and feeling like I was neglecting my own. There were very few nice kids in the school due to the arrogance of the army families, the prestigious mindset, and combined with the constant corruption within the administration, the time to leave was now. I looked at my kids that day and they knew something was wrong. They knew I was leaving. They had seen this happen so many times before. I had so many hugs that day from my kids and quite a few apologies from a few of them for not being better students, for not handing their work in on time, for not being good enough. The things they were apologising for was heartbreaking. When I told them that they had nothing to apologise for, everything was going to be OK, I had a moment of weakness. Was I doing the right thing? Then I saw Dalia's face through the window, just glaring at me. Then Mai appeared, then Reham. The kids looked scared and worried. Omar asked me, "Miss, what's going on?" I told him I wasn't sure, but he should get on with his work, they were probably just assessing me. "Well I hope they give you a gold star Miss because you're the best teacher we've ever had."

Dalia opened the door and came in, told me to gather my things from the staff room, I was leaving. Mai and Reham looked so smug. One of the other teachers was stood sheepishly behind them both, head bowed and as I walked out, she walked in. The kids were asking, "What's going on? Where are you going Ms Dawn? Ms Dawn don't go! Why are you so mean to Ms Dawn?"

Hamza piped up, "Because she's the best teacher we've ever had and that the school had ever had and they are jealous, that's why!" I turned to him and just smiled at him, gave him a wink and told them all to be the very best they could be, remember they can do anything they set their minds to and that I loved them all.

Khaalid saw me being taken from my classroom, and knew this was the end. I went up to the staffroom and handed over the work books that I had created for the kids in my class, telling Reham that there was three months' worth of work inside those packs, all with assessments, homework and extension work. I then handed her all the receipts for the books I had already taken back to the pitiful library and said I was ready to go. She looked shocked. She realised in that moment I had planned to walk, but not leaving my kids without work to do. I had even created a teacher's guide for the next teacher and a full report on each child so they knew where each child was and what their strengths, weaknesses and personality traits were. They were great kids and I was going to miss them. Not as much as I missed my kids in FS1, that broke my heart, but these kids deserved so much more than they had been getting. I walked out of the staffroom and to Khaalid's class, he had already packed his bag when he's seen me walk past with Reham, as he'd seen them all standing outside of my classroom. He walked out of his classroom and we went and got Naasir.

Naasir had forgotten a couple of his books, so I went into the class and got the books. At this point the male supervisor grabbed me and pushed me to the floor, telling me I had no right to these books. I got up and told him, "I think you'll find I do, I paid for them." Khaalid had picked up the books, and the three of us walked out of the school. I had been timing this exit perfectly as I had been paid a week before, and so it seems had the school.

It wasn't the exit I had planned. I had planned for it to be done at the end of the school day, and certainly not in front of the kids, but Dalia, Reham and Mai had other ideas. It didn't matter, I had all the things I needed to homeschool the boys and we were on our way home.

In the taxi the boys were both in the back with me giving me hugs. Khaalid, being Khaalid, told me he was proud of me and that I was not to worry. I kissed him on the top of the head and pulled him tighter towards me. Naasir was telling me that he hadn't liked the school ever since a little girl had been killed right outside, simply because her older sister had been too busy on her phone to take care of her whilst walking across the road. The male teachers and corridor supervisors pounced on the driver of the car as he got out to see what had happened, and they beat him senseless, then left him. All of this as the kids were leaving school. One girl dead, her sister, who was a few years older than her, taken to hospital critical, whilst the eldest sister was crying; and teachers and staff members beating up a guy when the accident had been the fault of the eldest sister stepping out in front of him. Bear in mind the road outside of the school was a very fast moving, triple carriage way and the school made no provisions to keep these kids safe, even though there were 1000's of them getting on buses, in cars and walking to the next junction to get a minibus home. The school didn't even acknowledge this girl had died. No assembly, no mention of it in class, just to carry on as normal. I was warned not to speak about it in class, which was incredibly difficult as they want to ask questions and when I told them we were not allowed to talk about it, they were upset even more. The school was rotten from the inside out and I was glad to be out of there, glad to get my boys out of there.

When we got home the boys rallied round, made me a cup of tea and put on a David Attenborough Blue Planet episode and said, "We're going to do science now mummy, you relax with your cup of tea." This made me giggle and cry all at the same time, because as I sat there and watched them watching Sir David Attenborough, I was thinking about the fact that so far we had been in Egypt less than three years and the boys had already been in three different schools. So much upheaval, taken away from friends they had made, and now the task of homeschooling was upon me. Was I up to it? Could I do this? Too bloody right I could! It was GAME ON time and I was more than ready to watch my children learn and enjoy being part of the process.

The delights of Homeschooling.

Homeschooling was becoming a growing trend amongst parents in Egypt who wanted their children to actually get somewhere and were willing to stand up against the 'normal' thing to do. I had the learning resource guides I had copied, and I had all the text books the boys had been using. I ordered a load of books from Sigrun and collected those. I enrolled my boys in at the Ma'adi music school to learn guitar and piano, we started taking Arabic lessons at U-Can every day, and the boys joined a Tai Kwon Do class just around the corner from where we lived. During this last week I was due to see the parents again and sitting there knowing I was leaving was very hard. The feedback the parents had given me was overwhelmingly positive. They told me that their child had never looked forward to school so much. That the progress they had made was so surprising, it wasn't possible. I had also created a plan of action for both of them, creating lesson plans around the same subject as an activity and then set them the exercises in their own books to complete. They were 4 years apart and yet they were absorbing and learning from each other. It worked. I split them up and gave one of them reading time, or maths time, whist the other worked with me on a different task so I could focus on the more complex stuff for Khaalid or extend Naasir's grasp ready to do the next level with Khaalid. Khaalid loved being able to help Naasir, but Naasir being an independent soul was refusing the help.

Hearing their ideas, their thought processes was an amazing gift. I had seen other children learning, and I had of course seen my boys learn things around the house and whilst they were both preschool age, but this, this whole process of seeing my boys learn, capture, internalise and express for themselves, a very beautiful experience. Yes I worried about them losing out on the social skills but I was also worried about the social skills they would have picked up had we stayed in EBIS. Did I regret leaving Narmer? In part, yes, but only because of the gardens and the location. Out of the three schools it was the better one, but it was the emotional intelligence that let them down, but then again the whole country lacked emotional and social intelligence so it was not surprising that the schools didn't have it.

Sometimes the boys and I would go to The Bookspot and get their new resources, stop off at Mugshot and have lunch. We'd stay there for hours doing art, history, geography whatever was planned for that day. We went to a place called Fagnoon in Giza, an amazing place! There was wood working, metal work, glass painting, assault courses, herb gardens and a whole host of other activities that they could enjoy. The boys loved it. We would have our lessons on a felucca, take a packed lunch and just enjoy ourselves. I often wondered why I hadn't done this before. It really had made such a difference to our lives. ramO stepped in and did some maths and science with the boys as my book was finally going to print. I was able to do a lot more with JCI and tutor more kids so I was kept busy.

Noha and I met up regularly as she lived nearby. We had dinner together, she would teach the boys some lessons as she had also left EBIS, also in a blaze of glory. Lisa had left after a month of meeting her, but we'd remained in contact so the three of us would get together for coffee. Noha and I would go to the Jazz club and she also knew Osama and Yehya. I confided in her about where I was at with regards to Islaam and she got it. I told her just lately all I could smell was wine. I wanted to have a drink. It had been 15 years since I had had any alcohol and so we planned a night in together where it was just her and I, I wanted to do this with someone I trusted and not with ramO. I wanted to do this for me, and only me. I also told her I didn't want to wear the scarf anymore and she said I had to do what felt right, so I walked back to my apartment without it on. I started to wear hats. I also went to Pace e Luce in Ma'adi to see Nora, and told her that I wanted Toni Eissa to restyle my hair. They listened, they got where I was at and he worked his magic. It felt amazing, looked amazing and where I had walked in with the scarf on, I left without it. I turned up at Noha's for dinner a few days later and we sat there looking at the wine list for Drinkie's – the only place you could buy alcohol, other than in International hotels. I was going through the wine list, cross checking the vineyards, the soil type and the grape content. Noha laughed at me and I said, "Well if you think I am drinking crap wine after 15 years of not drinking, you're bonkers!!"

She replied, "It's Egypt Dawn, it's all going to be crap wine!" We laughed so much that night even before the wine turned up and when it did, I savoured it. We polished off two bottles between us and I felt great. No hangover in the morning, just up and at 'em as usual. I wore the scarf less and less, and then one night ramO and I were heading out to the Cairo Jazz club with our long-time friends Deena and Ehab. I loved these two people so much, but we hardly ever saw them. Ehab was always working away and Deena was dealing with three kids and the family business. Our conversations were always passionate, deep and full of laughter. Beautiful people.

Ehab and Deena were shocked but not shocked when they saw me without the scarf. Ehab said, "We'll talk later," with a mischievous grin on his face. We drank Baileys, the first time I had had Baileys in 15 years, oh it was divine! How I had missed it. We then did shots and danced the night away. It was fab!

A couple of weeks later Noha and I went to a pet shop to collect some cat feed for a cat she was taking of for the animal sanctuary she was volunteering at. When we went in I was appalled at how the 'pets for sale' were kept. The cages were piled high on top of one another, too many dogs per cage and their toilet business dropping through from one cage into another. I wanted to buy all of them and take them home and love them. The boys had been wanting a dog for ages. ramO was coming around to the idea and I knew this was the right time to get one. The boys and I were home most of the day, and it just felt right. I was smitten by two fluffy white dogs, but I had always had big dogs, so was torn. With living in an apartment, the smaller toy dog would be better, so as soon as Noha and I had finished what we were doing we, said goodbye and I walked back to my apartment and I told ramO about the puppies. I told him he had to come and see them. The boys were at their Arabic lessons for the next 20 minutes so we had enough time to go and get the dog and surprise them when they got home. He relented. We were going to get a puppy!!! I was ecstatic!! I had grown up with dogs and had missed having one, but life wasn't conducive to having a dog before now. When we got back to the pet shop, one of the white fluffy dogs had gone and the other one was left, looking really sad. I wanted him. So we questioned the pet shop worker, which took longer than we expected, paid our deposit, then went to get the boys. We didn't tell them what we were doing but we grabbed a bag and a blanket and took them with us. The boys were trying to guess what we were up to, getting excited. When we walked into pet shop and walked to the dogs at the back, they got really excited and said, "Walaahi?? We're getting a puppy?!"

ramO said yes, and he was already smitten with the white fluff ball. I took the puppy out of the cage he was in, and he couldn't stop licking my hand. The boys wanted to hold him and so our new addition to the family passed from one to the other. He kept looking back at me though, well it had been the third time he had seen me and I had just taken him out of this filthy cage. He was only two months old and absolutely adorable. We discussed what to call him over dinner and Kelt was chosen as we thought he was a Scottish terrier, or that is what we were told he was. After we had cleaned him up and taken him to the vet to get all his vaccinations, and his microchip, sorted he looked more like a Maltese. We then discovered he was a Lhasa Apso. It didn't matter what he was, he was ours. He was very underweight and due to the cold at night, he slept with ramO and I in the bed just so we could keep him warm, otherwise the cold would have killed him. He was so tiny, and he loved our terrapin Monster. He would follow him with such fascination, and if Monster stuck his head out of his shell, Kelt would run away.

One day whilst our maid was cleaning Kelt got hold of the feather duster and tried to run off with it, but the head of the duster was twice the size of him and it was hilarious to watch. The boys created a project about Kelt, doing research, learning the history, the geography of where the breed Lhasa Apso had come from, health problems, weights, heights etc and they smashed so many learning objectives with that project without them even knowing about it. They watched Ceasar Milan the Dog Whisperer and started teaching him tricks, but it was me he wanted. Me he followed everywhere. He was my dog. When it came for him to go for his rabies shot, I took him to the vet, who had been recommended to us and the shot was given.

In the next 48 hours I saw Kelt become withdrawn and his stools had become really loose. Then he just started bleeding from his backend, from his mouth, eyes, nose everywhere. I was really worried and I knew there was a vet just next door to U-Can on Rd 199 and took Kelt to see them immediately. Dr Ramy examined Kelt and did some tests, told me Kelt had Parvo. I had never heard of it, but what I was about to find out scared me. We hadn't even had this little fella six months and there was no way he was going to die. Not on my watch. Dr Ramy told me Kelt would have to stay in overnight to be observed and drip fed. I said, "No way. I am going to take him home with me, and you are going to give me all the liquids, meds and equipment I need to take care of him, or you are going to allow me to stay here overnight, every night until he is better."

Dr Ramy beamed at me and called through his assistant who got all the drips and meds, Kelt needed. He inserted the catheter and showed me how to change the fluids and meds. He talked me through what I should be watching for and told me to give Kelt finger tips of honey and labneh, a rich thick yoghurt drink. The boys were really worried when I got back. Naasir sat on the couch to hold Kelt and Khaalid helped me and ramO set up the equipment and I showed him what Dr Ramy had shown me to do. Khaalid wanted to help, so did Naasir, but due to Naasir's age, I wasn't going to let him change the meds through the catheter.

The next few weeks were touch and go. I stayed up throughout the night to hold Kelt, make sure he didn't stop breathing, or vomited and messed all over himself. Holding his fragile little body in my arms was heart breaking, and the thought of leaving him alone in the vets overnight was unimaginable. Who does that? Just leave their pets to die alone in a cold and sterile place? Not me that's for sure! Dr Ramy called every morning to check on Kelt and after the first week, I took Kelt back to see him. He was really pleased with his progress. He changed the catheter and kept him on the meds but told me to try him on some chicken and rice blended up like a soup.

After another week, we added liver to that mix to build up his strength. He was growing stronger and we were able to then remove the catheter. Kelt had become one of the 10% of dogs that survived Parvo, and Dr Ramy credited that to me and the boys for nursing him at home in a loving environment. Kelt knew he was loved and that was all part of the healing process.

Kelt went everywhere with us after that. He came to The Bookspot, restaurants and he even came with me to U-Can for my lessons, and whilst I was teaching because Hanaan, Laurice and Peter had fallen in love with him. Another teacher there, Heather, I had met before through another friend

Lilia, and it was a pleasure to see her again. We caught up and she shared some of the horror stories she and other friends had encountered at different schools across Cairo. What I had experienced in both Narmer and EBIS was so common place it was scary. How on earth did Egypt expect to thrive when schools were this toxic?

Lessons at U-Can were fun and I really loved Laurice being my teacher. I had lessons with an older couple from the states who just decided to travel and learn languages as they went. I couldn't believe they were over 65 the pair of them.

Our home was a relatively happy home, although ramO and I were finding it hard to communicate about certain things due to not wanting the boys to overhear. Things were kicking off again, and it was clear that the old regime wanted to overthrow Morsi. Was it all going to happen again? Only time would tell. ramO was hardly ever home due to the continued work with the BBC and Wamda the online tech-entrepreneur magazine, and we were both writing for AUC again, even though they were still far behind on payments. JCI was doing well and growing and we were making headway with member awareness. After a shaky start we had a strong team of people working on the growth strategy that I had put in place. Some people were put off because we had a niqaabi on our team but she was so good, she could have worn a potato sack over her head and I would have still wanted her on the team. I just couldn't get my head around why so many were discriminating against others based on their clothing choice and beliefs when they were clearly the obvious person for the job in hand. I was very proud of the progress Mahmoud had made since the first night I had met him. He had grown so much, travelled more and more overseas seeking out other JCI events, was networking, creating Facebook pages and events for JCI Egypt and JCI Cairo. More and more people were turning up to the events but they were just not being converted into members… because they couldn't afford the membership fee. They were stuck in the mindset that it was an expense rather than an investment. They were happy to spend money on coffee and lunches, with a shisha at Beano's, Cilantro or Costa, but not willing to spend the same amount per month in learning and developing their skills. I've never understood it. If you would rather invest in a company's profits by drinking coffee or eating out, but you are not prepared to spend that money in investing in your own knowledge and growth, then that's up to you, but why would you do that? Do you value the company's growth over your own? Obviously, you do. Me? I value myself and my growth, so give me knowledge and growth over a pair of Jimmy Choos any day, because one day I'll be able to afford dozens of them AND still invest in my knowledge!

Around about April time, ramO and I took Khaalid to the dentist. He needed to have his tongue tie cut so that he could speak Arabic better by being able to roll his 'R', as well as all the additional added benefits of being able to stick your tongue out, lick an ice cream for example. ramO had asked for it to be done in the UK, but because Khaalid spoke English eloquently they refused to do it, even though it was hindering his ability in Arabic. ramO was told about the process and when we arrived they then went through it again with us all after re-examining Khaalid's mouth. They told us that it would just be a local anaesthetic, no stitches and we'd be out in 20 minutes. Three hours later, some 12 injections later and over 20 stitches, I was furious. Not only had I passed out twice due to the amount of blood, but Khaalid had been sat in a chair for three hours with his mouth wide open whilst these two butchers, with blood all over their hands, repeatedly dived into Khaalid's mouth to do what we were told was a very simple procedure; this was done by the most highly recommended dentist in Cairo.

They wanted to charge us 1000LE (£100) instead of the 200LE. I told them they were getting nothing. Shocked they questioned me why I was not willing to pay them. "Not willing to pay you? Why the hell should I after what you have just put my son through, and us through? You lied about the process and you are now expecting payment? I don't think so!"

Their only response was, "Well, if we had told you how long and what was really involved you wouldn't have done it."

"What the fuck??" was the first words out of my mouth, "Are you for real? Walaahi? You just actually said that? So you violated our human rights of being able to make an informed decision and give our child the correct information to prepare him just because you think we are as stupid as you are? You're thieves, and corrupt, just like the rotten government overthrown in February two years ago. No wonder Egypt is broken. Ya rabbi[57]! Haram!" I walked out with the boys, and told ramO that if he paid them, he was part of the problem, and not to bother trying to explain himself.

---

57   Ya rabbi! – my God!

I was done. I was completely done. I wanted to go home to England. I had had enough of Egypt and didn't want to raise my children here. I didn't want them to grow up in a toxic, ignorant and corrupt country such as this.

Things had been strained between ramO and I due to all the pressures we'd been facing. We'd had a few fights and I just put it all down to the outside stresses. We talked about going home to England and then when the military coup happened and Morsi was overthrown in June, that was it, I was not staying any longer. I told ramO to book flights and if he wanted to stay he could stay, but the boys and I were going. He was reluctant but he agreed. We were going home.

Going home.

ramO went to see his mum and told her the news and she instantly put the house we had lived in, on the market. She was selling the house from underneath us. What I had been led to believe about the house ownership was completely false. It wasn't trusted to us and the boys to avoid inheritance tax and she was completely in her rights to sell. So now I was tasked with looking for a house to live in.

She promised us a certain amount from the sale of the house, especially considering we had invested over £100,000 in the house over the last 12 years of living there, so that would be a great deposit on a house, and it was a new start for us, even though I loved the house we lived in, especially the garden.

I let all my friends know I was leaving in October, as well as all my students and the team at U-Can. One of the mums of one of the young girls I tutored asked me to be mean to her daughter from now on so when the time came for me to leave she wouldn't be as upset. I couldn't believe what this mother was asking me to do. Why on earth would I be mean to a child? Walaahi, there was some really messed up thinking going on, and to so many in Egypt is considered normal. Well, so happy not to be normal, especially if it means being nasty and spiteful.

Yasmine, Sarah and I all got the kids together and we went out to BillyBees on 6th October, left the kids to play for the next couple of hours and had coffee, ordered dinner next door to Billy Bees and whilst the order was being cooked, we went and got the kids. They had had a brilliant time. I made it my mission to really enjoy the last few months in Egypt, in amongst the promotion of my first book *Friday Bridge*, doing a few remaining events for JCI and having leaving parties.

I knew I would miss the iftars that I had so thoroughly enjoyed with friends, either at their homes or in ours. I was disappointed that other friends I had hoped to get to know better such as Tina, who was from Greece. I was going to miss Suzanna and her red heels, quirky and eccentric ways and most of all the love and support she gave to me and the boys. She could tell things were strained between ramO and I, but again, we all put it down to life in Egypt. Even Rowaida had told me to not assess my marriage whilst in Egypt. So I didn't. I let the insults, the criticisms and the aggression slide. ramO had seen a hell of a lot more violence and despicable things going on in Egypt than I had. Little was I to know what was coming next, nothing could have prepared me for what I was about to experience.

Ra'baa

On 14 August 2013, a month after Morsi had been removed from office, the Egyptian security forces raided two camps of protesters, one was at al-Nahda Square and the other one at Rabaa al-Adawiya Square. There had been talk that these were terrorist camps and that there was some really dodgy dealings going on. This was Egypt, of course there were! But what wasn't shown was the festival mood and facilities that were there. There were bouncy castles and water slides, there were lots of families having peaceful protests, barber shops, people were even filming from inside the camps, basically the majority were just camping out in support of Morsi. There were a few yobs, but show me a festival anywhere around the world that doesn't have idiots trying to spoil it for everyone. Both camps were occupied by supporters of President Mohamed Morsi, Yes there had been lots of protests against him, but to be fair, I actually agreed with a lot of what he was trying to do. He wanted to step away from USAid so Egypt could learn to stand on its own two feet, without beingtold what to do by America. He wanted to rebuild Egypt and the improvements he'd already made were noticeable. Really noticeable. The streets weren't as littered, although that was going to take time. Electricity cuts weren't happening as often and there was a lot less harassment on the streets.

ramO had been down the camps with the BBC, and many of my friends either had friends camping down there, or had been down there. Not because they supported Morsi perse, but because they were against the fact that the military had overthrown the first democratically elected President in 5000 years. That actually meant something to a lot of people; and a lot of people were angry. Really angry. People had died in Tahrir protesting for democracy in Egypt. People had lost their sons, fathers, brothers in the protest and now the military had decided to overthrow the president? Of course they should be pissed off! Of course they should be at one of these camps in objection to what had happened. If they didn't go, if they didn't protest, then those lives meant nothing.

The intimidation to those in the camps was gentle at first and then the beltagi came out in full force again; and the police brutality. There had been initiatives to end the six week sit-ins but they had failed to remove the people, but nothing had worked the people still remained. So they brought in the big guns, quite literally as well. They were using the excuse that those within the camps were killing others, they were dangerous and that it was inciting violence and caused a national security threat.

It felt like January and February two years earlier, but more sinister. We knew what the military were really capable of this time around. We'd seen the way they had worked, and we'd also seen how the police worked. Driving their armoured vehicles into people, mindless killing of innocent protestors. I didn't want the boys to see any of it, so I didn't have the TV on, other than for us to watch history and science documentaries or films together. The energy was changing again and I didn't like it.

We'd already seen many guys that had worn beards for years, start shaving. I had already witnessed women in niqaab being dragged off the street and beaten. One woman, I couldn't see what they were doing to her, but I could hear it, and I could hear her screams. Seeing her dragged away from her children like that and them just being left crying whilst the police dragged her off, was probably one of the scariest things I had seen yet. A bawaab and his wife rushed to the aid of the children, and I just stood there. I couldn't move. I was on my way to meet ramO and the boys from their swimming lessons, and I just couldn't move.

Another woman who had seen it, and was obviously numb to seeing this kind of thing, asked me if I was okay. How do you answer that? How do you even know if you are okay? I just nodded, and said thank you, before walking off in the direction of the swimming pool. I stopped at Volume One stationary shop because they had a coffee shop there and I just needed to kind of hide somewhere safe. I loved stationary and as I walked around the shop I came to the gift section and there was a massive teddy bear. I picked it up and held it so tightly, pushing my face into it and wishing I could unsee and unhear what I had just seen and heard. I put the bear down and breathed deeply, then I went and got my coffee, before walking to the pool.

I didn't get a chance to tell ramO what had happened because he had received a call that he needed to go to do some work with the BBC. So off he went and I was left with the boys to walk home. To walk past where no more than 30 minutes earlier I had been witness to such an awful event, and in Ma'adi Degla of all places.

I asked the boys if they wanted to go to Crave for dinner, and of course they said yes, they loved Crave. It was going to be one of the last times we would be there so I just told them to knock themselves out and order whatever they wanted. Khaalid noticed I was a bit distant, and asked if I was okay. Bless him, he always knew there was something wrong, even when I put on a brave face about things. Wise boy my Khaalid.

What was about to unfold in Rabaa al-Adawiya was unprecedented, so much so the events were described by Human Rights Watch as "one of the world's largest killings of demonstrators in a single day in recent history". According to Human Rights Watch, a minimum of 817 people and more likely at least 1,000 were killed in Rabaa Square on August 14.

The Egyptian Health Ministry of course didn't report numbers as high as HRW, coming in at 638, of which 595 were civilians and 43 police officers. There was bloodshed everywhere, police beltagi everywhere, just shooting, slaying people with machetes, throwing petrol bombs into groups of people, Bulldozers were sent in earlier in the day to clear the camps, but they didn't just clear the camps of tents and the material items in the camps, they bulldozed people over and killed them. They used snipers on roof tops to kill anyone that was in the vicinity, almost like they were playing down at a 'tin can alley' shooting range. Friends were posting video footage, sending text messages, photos, news updates constantly. ramO was out with the protests that were taking place in response to the violence against this peaceful protest, and what was fast becoming a bloody massacre. The total amount of casualties made 14 August the deadliest day in Egypt since the uprising started in 2011. Many were calling what had happened back then a revolution, but it wasn't; these actions simply proved it. I was mortified by what I was seeing and couldn't wait for October to arrive. I didn't know whether news had reached him yet as to what was happening, but before I got chance call him, he messaged me to let me know he was fine. I didn't hear from him for hours. I had no idea where he was, who he was with and I was afraid.

I had already heard from friends that homes were being raided of those involved in reporting, blogging or protesting; as well as those foreigners trying to leave the country.

As I had been followed several times by the secret police, which were not that secret, I was worried it would be my door that would be smashing in next. What had I done? What risks had I put my family in? What was I doing? And what would they do to me knowing I didn't consider myself a Muslim anymore?

They'd recently raided the home of a friend's brother-in-law in the middle of the night and dragged him, his family and his brother's family out of the beds, smashing up the homes, laughing whilst they were doing it. Then they left. That was the least I could probably expect.

I hadn't made it clear to anyone, not even ramO that I didn't want to be Muslim anymore. I think he maybe guessed as I had stopped wearing the scarf, was wearing short sleeve tops and not praying anymore in the traditional Islaamic sense of the word prayer. It wasn't that I didn't believe in God, it wasn't that I didn't believe in the Prophet Mohammed, but I just didn't see why, when all religions espoused pretty much the same things, all wanted peace, all spoke of being kind, giving to charity and being the best version of yourself, creating communities. So if they all said the same thing, and I resonated with so much of each one, on a higher more spiritual level than just the practical daily rituals, how could I call myself a Muslim? I was all of them surely? But I was also none of them. I was me, and I didn't want the label of religion to define me or my actions. I would define me and my actions. I would live in the current world, with the current knowledge and keep learning, keep evolving and I didn't need a religion to do that. I just needed a brain, a big heart and a longing for peace, coupled with my pure intentions to be good, kind and humble; to always do my best and be the best version of me I could possibly be.

But how do you explain that to people so stuck in the mindset of full on power and control, rigid thinking that meant they didn't even challenge the Qur'raan when even in the Qur'raan it says, "Do not follow your fore fathers blindly," and "There is no compulsion in religion." Here were two verses from the Qur'raan that had given me strength as I'd gone through this evolution of self and understanding of what it meant to be human over the last three years.

ramO still wasn't home by midnight, I told the boys he'd gone to stay at a friend's house because the roads were blocked, which they were, but I had no idea where he was. I was staying awake checking for his Facebook posts to pop up, or a text message. I just couldn't go to sleep knowing he was out there somewhere, not knowing whether he was dead or alive. So I wrote a blog post about what I was feeling, the fears, the anxiety, but no mention of leaving Islaam. No one was going to know. Not yet. I wasn't ready to go public, especially as converting to Islaam had put me in the spotlight in the bloody first place.

About 1am I got a call from ramO. I burst into tears just hearing his voice. Knowing the man I had fallen further in love with over these last few years, the father of my boys, was safe. When he told me he couldn't get back due to the road blocks I giggled and said, "That's what I told the boys before they went to bed." Then I just started crying. He was safe. My man was safe. I could sleep now. So we said goodnight and see you tomorrow.

He arrived home the next day to a roast dinner, and I'd also made gluten free sticky toffee pudding, Nigella styleee! When he walked through the door, all four of us ran to him, the boys, Kelt and me. It was a moment I will never forget. I kissed him so hard. Then slapped him on the top of the arm, and said, "Don't do that to me again, okay?"

He pulled me tighter into his arms and said he wouldn't. The boys hugged us both tightly and were cheering "family hug, family hug" then we all laughed, hugged a bit more and then whilst ramO freshened up I took lunch out of the oven ready to plate up.

Over the next few days, violent retaliation followed all over Cairo. ramO was out with the BBC again and the interim government declared a month-long state of emergency and we had curfews again. This time though, if you were out after curfew, you were thrown into the back of an armoured police car and taken to who knows where, and had who knows what done to you.

Nothing had changed, only the dark depths of evil getting darker and deeper. Egypt wasn't going to change, and it was very clear that Stockholm syndrome was well and truly in place in the psyche.

I was glad to be leaving. Noha was leaving too, Lisa had already left. Rowaida was leaving, so was Gitanjeli and Mahmoud couldn't wait to leave.

Packing up the home was a great focus, I would miss so many elements of Egypt, my friends of course, sailing on what had been deemed as my felucca by the men down at the felucca station. I would miss my students, I would miss sitting on my balcony reading in the warmth, but as I was going through the list of things I would miss, I hit a block. What else about Egypt would I really miss? The deliveries of anything you could possibly want delivered to your door at any time day or night. I wouldn't miss the family because in the three and a half years we had been there, we had only seen the extended family twice and the mother-in-law maybe nine times? And that was fine by me.

I had loved Egypt, but I had seen the ugly side of it, and that had tainted my view. I loved the people that were striving to create a better Egypt, such as Mazen Helmy at The District, Adam at iceCairo and of course Mahmoud with his never ending missions. I hoped that there were many more that.

Under different circumstances, I would have achieved more here in Egypt, but I was left wondering whether I had set my kids in schools up to fail. Teaching them a different mindset, making such a positive difference in their lives, knowing that outside of my classrooms, Egypt was still Egypt. People pushed you. Men harassed women. Do well and others destroy you. A corrupt and spiteful society, with an evil military with the vile Sisi now in power.

Yes, I was ready to leave. I was sorry to feel this way, but Egypt had broken me, but it had also released me and made me evolve, so for those two reasons, my love for Egypt remains.

I hope and pray Egyptians reclaim their country from the Military one day, but I don't hold out much hope, especially with the state of the education system, and the mentality of the people. Egypt needs a miracle. I hope it will get one. And soon.

Epilogue

Returning home to England was a very surreal process, it was like groundhog day. Sitting at my dining room table entering all the new books into excel, as I had done with Amira before I left brought me to tears. I knew she wouldn't be there when I arrived back, and I'd never see her again. Her passing away had hit me hard. I was blessed that during our last phone call we had laughed so hard we were both crying with laughter.

I was excited to see Debbie and Ali, Tina, Rob and Alan. I wanted to let rip on the dance floor like never before, allow all the negativity of the last three and a half years disappear into the ground through the beat of the techno bass line. But that would have to wait, I had to see my family first.

Getting Kelt back into the UK was no problem, and only because I flew into Amsterdam first. You see if you are going to bring your dog back into the UK, I suggest you fly in via Amsterdam, because instead of making you pay a stupid amount of money to be away from your dog for months on end whilst they are in quarantine, all you have to do is make sure your pets vaccinations are all up to date, they've been micro-chipped, had all their flea/tick and worming done, and had a set of blood tests done to make sure there are no signs of rabies.

You can then fly your beloved pet home using an airline that has a live animal cargo section, get passed by the Dutch authorities and then fly into the UK. Now, wouldn't it make sense if the British authorities just implemented the same rules? Or is that just a tad too simple? Booking into the hotel to dump my stuff, Kelt and I headed out. I needed to revisit some of my favourite places and introduce Kelt to a whole new world. With new smells, sights and temperature it must have been a sensory overload for the little fella. I found one of my favourite deli café's, ordered their avocado, crayfish and rocket salad with chunky chips, a glass of wine and enjoyed being back home in Europe. Kelt was treated to a piece of chicken and a nice bowl of fresh water. He was loving it!

I started giggling to myself as I walked down the street, there were no car horns, no gunfire, no street dogs, no rubbish and there were only a handful of people. I got really excited and let out a "YAY!!" and continued giggling to myself as I walked down the street. I don't think the grin could have gotten any bigger! Plus it was October, I had warm clothes on and I was walking outside – with a cold air nipping at my cheeks! Oh how I had missed the Northern European Autumns! It was the simple things I had missed, like being able to press the button and cross the road, knowing the cars would stop; being able to walk along without men cat calling me and grabbing me. Not seeing people walking around with Kalashnikovs and AK47s, not seeing tanks, but bicycles – with and without children in the child seats attached, and couples walking along holding hands everywhere.

The most amusing thing for me though was the amount of hair everywhere!! Having just been in Egypt and with the majority women with their hair covered, seeing women with their hair free flowing, and in some mad crazy colours and styles, well let's just say I had a lot to learn when it came to styling my hair from now on. Normally it is a choice of down or in a pony-tail, but not for much longer.

I then walked along to find a shop that I always frequented and found out it had changed hands. Whilst talking with the owners they were impressed with the fact I was flipping in and out of Arabic, even more impressed with the fact I had only just landed after three and a half years out there. They made me a nice cup of herbal tea and showed me their latest book collection… and oh how beautiful the photos were within it.

I walked for hours, just because I could. It was wonderful, and I was out way past my curfew! I had missed Amsterdam and I was determined to come back in the next 12 months. By myself.

I went back to my hotel room, and Kelt was so excited. He wasn't tired at all. Neither was I. I was on a high energy vibe and so Kelt and I played and wrestled for ages. I loved my dog so much, and if I had to say what the best thing to come out of Egypt was, it would have to be him.

The next day I trekked across to the ferry terminal, using European public transport. Kelt was about to experience efficient, clean public transport and then a ferry crossing to Harwich, England. It was great to be able to travel with him so easily, and once we got to the sea, my heart soared! I was going to go straight up on deck and just face into the wind, smell the salt sea air and just lose myself in it. My dream of living at sea kept coming back to me, in very unexpected ways. The crossing was what they said was rough, well I didn't think so. Yes we swayed a bit that was half the fun! Seeing nothing but sea all around me, other boat lights in the distance, I was transported back to my childhood of sleeping on the beach whilst dad was beach fishing and wanting to be out at sea. Falling asleep to the sound of the waves, just perfect! The only other sounds that beat that were the sounds of my boys heartbeats, them both breathing deeply whilst sleeping and their laughter.

Arriving back at the ferry terminal and hearing English everywhere was a bit mad to be honest. Having heard the majority of conversations around me in Arabic, or American for the last three and a half years and now hearing 'English English' was funny, because I now understood why people found regional accents in England funny and the neutral English, one that reminded them of James Bond. When I came out of the ferry terminal, my father was waiting, and then I heard "SURPRISE!!" and as I turned around, there were my boys, all three of them!

ramO had not stuck to the plan! He was supposed to be meeting me at my dad's before we travelled to my mums for my sister's wedding in three days! But here he was, at the ferry terminal. "Thought I'd surprise you," he said and gave me a huge kiss. We were home and already the tension between us had gone. It was amazing what leaving a hostile environment can do for you almost instantly.

The drive back to my dad's was an interesting one. I hadn't sat in the front of a car for a very long time, and certainly not on the left hand side of the car. I was also not used to the traffic coming in the directions it was coming in and I was as nervous as hell. My father told me I needed to get back behind the wheel of a car and soon. I agreed, told him to pull over and let me drive. To which he told me to behave and just enjoy the view. When I asked him what view it was pitch black, he said, "Exactly." No light pollution, no cities lights, just pitch blackness as we drove through the country lanes back home. My childhood home.

A few days later and I'm with my mum looking for clothes to wear to my sister's weeding, bearing in mind all I had were my Ugg boots, shib shib and trainers, and lots of summer clothes and one cardigan, oh and a dress that was knee length and without sleeves. Having not worn a dress this short for the best part of 20 years, I was a tad nervous, add heels the situation and you have a comedy sketch!

Still I found a nice pair of what were called wedge heels, to match my deep aubergine and chocolate hair, and then it was sorting the boys out. It was so strange listening to the local people, and seeing all these strange sights. People had tattoos all over their arms like a sleeve, or across their faces. They even had these big rings in their ears which had stretched the hell out of them. WTF?? Didn't get it then, don't get it now. Being at my sister's wedding was very strange. My estranged brother was there, and I would rather have not seen him, but you suck it up for family and I was too stunned by everything I was absorbing. Again so much hair!! And flesh!! Women in dresses that revealed their boobs, legs and arms, plus the piercings that people had in their faces, what had happened to the British in the three and a half years since we left? Hearing the real local accent was taking a lot of getting used to again and being out after dark, I kept thinking "We need to get home, curfew is coming up" A totally different sensation to Amsterdam. This was a sensory, emotional and mental overload and I had to leave.

The weeks and months that followed were all about resettling, but life was to throw me more and more curve balls than I could ever imagine. Four weeks after arriving home, ramO called to tell me Babaa had died in a freak rain storm whilst driving home. The bottom of my world fell out and I dropped to the floor. I loved that man so much. He had been my dad for 18 years, guided me more than both my father and step dad ever had. He may not have been my blood father or the one to raise me during childhood, but he raised and guided me through my adult life. I couldn't believe it.

With the next two curveballs to hit me, the mother-in-law sold the family home, refusing to let me in to get all our furniture, and refusing to give us our share of the sale, leaving me broke and homeless with my boys. That alone would have killed Babaa. I knew she was a spiteful woman but leaving her only grandchildren without a home, well that was just the lowest of the low. I couldn't stay at my fathers, and my relationship with my mother was better, ever since she saw me on CNN in Tahrir, and lived in fear of actually losing me. We were rebuilding and moving in back home after 20 years of being away, back in Friday Bridge, that was never going to happen. I had to be in Sheffield with the boys by January ready for them to start school, so the mission was on. Operation Find-a-Home the boys called it, and then they told me that they never wanted to see An'na[58] again; that was fine by me.

I told ramO I was looking for a home in one of the most rural areas of Sheffield, I didn't want to be in the city, or close by. I wanted fields, and a local park for the boys to go off and play in whenever they wanted to. Somewhere quiet. Green. Perfect. And I found one at the end of January, we moved in. I got the Noro Virus, and had never felt so poorly in my life, even when I was sick with Naasir, but then I was pretty much out of completely when I was sick with him. I was in and out of it for about three weeks, but still kept pushing through it. I had to get the boys sorted for school, and with ramO back in Egypt finishing off projects ready to return home to England in the middle of 2014, there was a lot to do. I was going to be starting my masters and a new business, and I had a lot of planning and development to do.

ramO was coming back every three weeks, helping out with stuff, we went to London to see some immersive theatre in London for Valentines Day, it was the first ever Valentine's we had celebrated together. He told me I deserved it after everything I had achieved. Plus our friend Georgia, who we'd met in Egypt, was performing – so that was a double bonus!

I cracked on with everything UK side, whilst ramO sorted stuff out in Egypt. I then got news that my book *Friday Bridge* was going to be displayed at the London Book Fair, so childcare arranged, hotel and train tickets booked and off I went to London in April.

I came back on the Friday, ready to tell ramO all about it on the Sunday when we collected him at the airport.

Later that afternoon, without warning, he told me he wanted a divorce. No talking about it, no warning, no nothing. After 18 years. He just wanted to walk away. So he did. Our marriage was over. Curveball number two that would have killed his dad.

In the May that followed, I was admitted to hospital because I'd found a lump in my breast.

Wallahi!???? Could the universe throw anything else at me?

---

58   An'na – Grandma in Turkish but also used by Egyptians.

Luckily for me it was benign, but the ironic thing is I was in hospital having the operation on my wedding anniversary.

The truly amazing thing about having the surgery was, for the last eight years I had no memory of Naasir's birth. I was too sick. I had something called HELLP Syndrome and I was fighting not just to save my own life, but Naasir's as well.

Lying on the theatre table, the lights, smells and environment brought back all the memories of Naasir's birth. I could remember him being given to me. I remembered kissing his head (completely out of it, but still kissing the top of his head), I remembered seeing ramO holding him just like he had Khaalid 12 years before. I had been blessed with the memories of Naasir's birth due to such a scary moment.

I smiled, cried and thanked God, and said Alhamdulilah[59], because it could have been worse, a lot worse. I just lived through worse. How much worse than that could it get?

---

59   Alhamdulialh – thanks to God.